ACTION

5. *Follow the BRISLEDITCH Guides*

- Be brief, be simple, be direct.

- Be clear, be human.

6. *Write Effectively*

- Dictate rough draft from outline.

- Scan your draft first.

- Edit your draft vigorously.

7. *Read Effectively*

- Preread the message first.

- Choose your reading speed.

- Read for the poker chip structure.

8. *Listen and Speak Effectively*

- Chart progress on Purpose Vector.

- Use your spare listening time.

- Listen for the poker chip structure.

- Watch for and use nonverbal signals.

- Plan and rehearse the formal talk.

Make Yourself Clear!

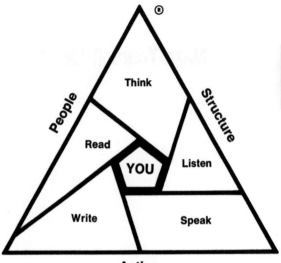

Make

Yourself Clear!

Morris on Business Communication

John O. Morris
Consultant in Management Communications

McGRAW-HILL BOOK COMPANY

New York   St. Louis   San Francisco   Düsseldorf   Johannesburg
Kuala Lumpur   London   Mexico   Montreal   New Delhi
Panama   Rio de Janeiro   Singapore
Sydney   Toronto

Library of Congress Cataloging in Publication Data

Morris, John O.
    Make yourself clear!

    1. Communication in management. I. Title.
HF5718.M66   658.4'5   77-39118
ISBN 0-07-043180-9

1 2 3 4 5 6 7 8 9 0   BPBP   7 6 5 4 3 2

The editors for this book were W. Hodson Mogan and Carolyn Nagy,
the designer was Naomi Auerbach, and its production
was supervised by Teresa F. Leaden. It was set in Alphatype Astro
by University Graphics, Inc.

It was printed and bound by The Book Press.

Contents

Preface

The Behind the Words system described in this book is based on practical experience. In 1964, I started my own firm; since then, as consultants in management communications, we have conducted workshops for thousands of managers and professionals using this system as a framework. At first, these workshops were limited to writing, but now they cover all communications—writing, speaking, reading, listening. This system has therefore been tested and improved through both the practical experience of these workshops and through the valuable postworkshop comments of participants.

The Behind the Words system can best be described as a synthesis of principles for effective communication which have been known at least since they were expressed by the Greek dramatists. This system, including its labels and arrangement, is my own; credit is given whenever I have specifically incorporated ideas of others. Cases and examples used to illustrate these principles are based on fact, but names and locales have been carefully disguised.

My interest in effective communication started during my school days with encouragement from my father to speak and write in simple, clear words. This interest continued at Yale, where I was an editor of the *Yale Daily News*. While at Virginia Law School, I realized that law cases were sometimes difficult to understand not because the legal concepts were difficult but because judges did not always write clearly. Later, at Aetna Life Insurance Company, I occasionally found myself distracted from a study of the issues involved in a problem by an awareness of the poor writing used to describe these issues.

My sincere thanks go to Ruth D. Grinnell, J. Read Murphy, and Lois L. Sinert, each of whom materially helped make this book a reality; and to my wife, Bernie, for her generous and unfailing support and encouragement.

JOHN O. MORRIS
West Hartford, Connecticut

Make Yourself Clear!

Poor Communications: an Increasing Problem

Introduction: the Morris Maxim

Are communications poor in most organizations?

Do many of the problems that face managers and professionals result from poor communications?

Are these problems of poor communications becoming increasingly serious?

All the evidence suggests that the answers to these questions are a clear yes. The inherent problem can be summarized by the Morris Maxim:

Communications problems grow much faster in any organization than the organization itself grows.

The hard facts that lie behind the Morris Maxim are these:
1. Managers and professionals do their jobs by communicating with people.
2. Our educators have not taught us how to communicate successfully.
3. The autocratic structure of an organization causes increasing communications problems as the organization grows.

3

4. Because of poor communications, senior managers of large organizations lose the power to change the mindless, relentless, onward movement of their organizations.

5. These communications problems daily become more serious because our increasingly complex world demands increasingly large organizations to manage it.

6. Improving communications is everyone's job; managers and professionals at all levels must
   - recognize the full implications of poor communications;
   - attack the problem repeatedly;
   - anticipate stubborn resistance to change.

Jean-Paul Sartre once said, "Hell is other people." In so saying, he dramatically summed up the communications problems that inevitably exist in every organization. You want to go one way; I want to go another. Through communication, we attempt to express, define, and reconcile our divergent views; sometimes we are successful; sometimes we are not. Sooner or later, the issue is decided; if you accept the decision openly and willingly, all is well; but if you resent the decision, consciously or subconsciously, conflict is created. If these conflicts increase on this or other issues, the organization's success in reaching its goals is gradually jeopardized. The process of expressing, defining, and reconciling can be difficult enough when only a few are involved; yet in the large organization, this process must take place between many people many times every day.

This book offers the Behind the Words system as a framework to help you, as an individual manager or professional, attack the problem of poor communications.

The remainder of this introduction comments in more detail on the six hard facts behind the Morris Maxim, and previews the Behind the Words system.

THE SIX HARD FACTS

1. Managers and professionals do their jobs by communicating with people.

This statement is almost self-evident. A production line worker in an automobile factory, a key punch operator in an office, a carpenter building a house, a mechanic adjusting a carburetor—each does his job with his hands.

A manager or professional on the other hand usually does his job by managing, directing, proposing, reporting, and persuading. His success is measured primarily by his ability to get results by working with and through other people; his ability to do this well is directly tied to his ability to communicate successfully. (Even the researcher must communicate the results of his work, before his task is complete.)

2. Our educators have not taught us how to communicate successfully.

Forward-looking educators have long been aware that our educational system fails to teach us to communicate successfully. This weakness starts at the elementary school level and carries through high school, college, and graduate school. The emphasis is principally on courses that teach us facts; seldom are courses in communications required, to teach us how to use these facts.

An occasional professor whose class is not too large may insist on a well-organized, carefully written essay; but objective exams, large, impersonal classes, and student graders make it easy to graduate with little or no training in the skills of effective communication.

Academia has too often scorned communications courses. The attitude has been that such courses teach skills and therefore are inferior to courses that teach facts. Sometimes those who were the most scornful were themselves the poorest communicators; in any case, this attitude ignores not only the problems created by poor communications but also the point that the ability to communicate well is a necessary, basic skill that we are not born with.

Successful communicators are made, not born. A child does not start life with the ability to write, read, speak, listen, and think successfully. These are skills he must learn as he grows up. Some learn faster than others, some become more skillful than others because of environment or innate ability, but all of us must learn the basic skills and techniques for communicating successfully.

3. The autocratic structure of an organization causes increasing communications problems as the organization grows.

Today's business organization or government agency is built on an autocratic pattern in which authority flows down through the organizational pyramid from those at the top. When large corporations and government agencies first began to make their appearance in the nineteenth century, the only other large organizations available as models were the Roman Catholic Church and the Army. Both organizations were rigidly autocratic, requiring obedience to orders from above and punishing disobedience with excommunication or court-martial.

The autocratic structure does not encourage effective vertical or lateral communications. The subordinate, fearful of being criticized, disciplined, or denied promotion by his superior, thinks twice before telling the superior anything that might not please him. The superior, on the other hand, enjoying his power and probably feeling that his knowledge or ability is greater, does not always take the trouble or time to listen to his subordinate and obtain his views; instead he simply issues orders. Lateral communications in the autocratic organization often present even greater problems. Managers at the same level, attempting to agree on a course of action, often view each other with suspicion, jealousy, fear, and outright hostility. The jockeying for position and the protection of carefully built mini-empires become more important than the issue itself.

Do these communications problems exist in organizations that have made serious efforts to adopt some of the newer approaches to organizational development and effective management? The answer must be yes, although hopefully to a lesser degree. The core of the problem is the extraordinary difficulty in getting people within an autocratic organization to communicate with each other openly. Until they do this, they cannot attack problems with full effectiveness.

The larger the organization, the more difficult it becomes to communicate successfully. In a five-man organization, all the members can, with luck, face their conflicts, establish their goals, and communicate openly with each other to their own greater benefit and to the benefit of their small organization. But how infinitely more difficult this becomes if those five people become, let us say, a unit in a 50,000-man organization. Now they must not only take into consideration their own conflicts and goals as they reach their decisions, but they must consider the effect of their decisions on others in their large organization.

Before they make decisions, they must now hold meetings with those who might be affected; they must discuss, coordinate, listen to those with opposing views, listen to those who simply oppose change, write or read memos for and against their approach, and finally reach and communicate a result that somehow balances conflicting views and pressures. The process is all too familiar to any manager or professional in any large organization—private or public.

Furthermore, all the communications that are necessary to reach a basic decision in themselves present further communications problems; meetings must be scheduled and efficiently run; memos must be edited and reviewed, conflicts as to how to present a particular viewpoint must be reconciled. What might have been a simple decision has thus become a complex problem, involving too much time of too many people.

All this leads to the deadly disease of paper work proliferation, chronic in every large organization. Reports pour upstream to senior managers; instructions, procedures, and directives flow at an ever-increasing rate downstream to lesser managers and the rank and file; reports and instructions move back and forth laterally. Too many people spend too much of their time preparing, monitoring, editing, coordinating, reviewing, and just plain reading or attempting to read all this mass of paper.

After a while, people run out of time and interest and simply stop reading. This has already happened in some giant corporations and federal agencies, where managers cannot find time to intelligently read the plethora of paper work that fills their in-boxes every day.

4. *Because of poor communications, senior managers of large organizations lose the power to change the mindless, relentless, onward movement of their organizations.*

This is a frightening fact, but it is inescapable. Presidents of large corporations and heads of major government agencies are acutely aware of the extraordinary difficulty of producing real change within their own organization—whether this change involves a new product, service, or program; the cleaning up of inefficiency; or an effective response to change from outside.

When a giant bureaucracy (private or public) has established a pattern of moving in a certain direction, a mindlessness sets in. Whether or not the movement in that direction was started by accident or on purpose, whether or not the reasons for so moving were valid when started but are no longer valid now, change becomes an appallingly difficult task.

Change becomes so difficult because many of the people

who must accept the change will instinctively and automatically oppose it. Many people, particularly those in the middle of the organization, will see no advantages to them personally from the change. Change represents a threat; hence they fear it and resist it. In the small organization, the change makers may be able to communicate individually with each of these people, but in the large organization, this has become impossible. Change therefore becomes increasingly difficult in the large organization because so many people are involved in the change; so many people will resist it and must be persuaded not to oppose it; so many communications are required to gather facts, persuade people, and make and carry out decisions; and, finally, because so many people involved in this complex process do not know how to communicate successfully.

5. *These communications problems daily become more serious because our increasingly complex world demands increasingly large organizations to manage it.*

It would be nice indeed if we could return to an era of smaller, simpler, and more controllable organizations, but we cannot. The federal government, whether we like it or not, will continually increase its powers because so many major problems (such as welfare, ecology, and inner-city ghettos) can apparently only be handled effectively by giant agencies at the federal level. Large corporations are constantly gobbling up smaller ones; the diversity of talents, products, services, and markets and the greater financial strength of the giant corporation all combine to help it succeed in a way the smaller corporation cannot.

6. *Improving communications is everyone's job; managers and professionals at all levels must*
- *recognize the full implications of poor communications;*
- *attack the problem repeatedly;*
- *anticipate stubborn resistance to change.*

The purpose of this book is to present the Behind the Words

system as a framework to help you, as a manager or professional, attack the problem. Like most serious problems, we cannot successfully attack it on all frontiers simultaneously, but each of us in our own way can start the process of change—first within ourselves and then within those who will listen to us.

To do this, first, we must recognize that the problem exists—this is in itself difficult because we have all lived with it so long that we often fail to see it; second, we must make up our minds to launch a determined attack at every level, including our own personal level; third, we must be prepared for the inevitable stubborn resistance to change, both in ourselves and in others.

This book is particularly written for you, therefore, if you are ready to start this process of change.

The Behind the Words System: a Preview

The Behind the Words system collects and organizes the basic principles for effective management communications into an orderly system, easily learned and easily remembered.

This system recognizes that these basic principles are similar, whether you are listening, speaking, writing, reading, or thinking. It therefore applies across the board to all types of communications. The system is illustrated by the triangle below:

In this triangle:
- YOU are in the center;
- You listen, speak, write, read, and think within the *People-Structure-Action* framework.

People are the human relations side of the triangle; Structure is the organizing side; Action is the doing side. The name "Behind the Words" helps remind us of the work necessary for successful communications before we speak or write.

The four basic types of communications are listening, speaking, writing, and reading, illustrated by four of the five sides of the pentagon inside the triangle. Thinking is included as the fifth side because orderly thinking is a necessary condition to any type of successful communications.

This is a system to help you as a manager or professional communicate more effectively on the job. (To avoid repetition of the words "manager" or "professional" in the remainder of this book, a professional will be assumed to be a manager.) Some of the principles for communicating effectively on the job are the same or similar to those for communicating effectively anywhere, but some are different. For example:

1. Your audience is reading or listening for meaning when you write or speak. You are not a novelist, a TV star, or a newspaper reporter. Your audience is therefore reading or listening not for general information, not to admire the polished perfection of your prose, not to be entertained by your story; rather, they want to know what action, if any, they should take as a result of your message.

2. As the sender of the message, you almost always seek some form of action or results from your audience. Again, your purpose is not merely to entertain, amuse, or even to inform.

3. Your time is limited; your audience's time is limited. This is on-the-job communications.

4. You communicate as part of an organization. You must follow precedents and seek approvals, up and down. Sometimes precedents are out of date and stultifying; sometimes the pressures to conform do not allow you the

freedom you would like. But you may have more freedom than you think, because some of the obstacles you fear do not really exist; they are myths developed to justify the status quo.

The principles of the Behind the Words system, summarized in the remainder of this introduction, are listed in the inside front and back covers of this book. You may find it helpful to refer to these from time to time.

In the Behind the Words system, People, Structure, and Action are the main ideas (referred to as "blue chips"). Subordinate to these are the eight numbered steps (referred to as "red chips"); subordinate in turn are the guides collected under each step (referred to as "white chips").

In the game of poker, the blue chips are worth the most, followed by the red chips and then the white chips. By analogy, therefore, the most important ideas in any message are the blue chips. Subordinate to the blue chip ideas in importance are the red chip ideas, and subordinate to the red chip ideas are the white chip ideas. This analogy is used throughout the Behind the Words system.

PEOPLE

The first main, or blue chip, heading of the Behind the Words system, and thus the first side of the Behind the Words triangle, is People. Under this heading are collected the key steps and guides concerning the human relations side of communicating.

Step 1   Ask the Three People Questions

The guides under this step are worded as questions:
- What is your purpose?
- Who is involved?
- What do they want?

If you don't know what you want or why you are communicating, you are not likely to succeed. This is obvious but sometimes ignored. If you begin to talk or write before you have thought out your purpose, your message will probably show a lack of direction. In short, know where you are going before you start.

Next, stop and consider all the other people involved in this communication. For example, if you are writing a report, who else will read it besides the named addressees? What do you known about them? What is their environment? What do they mean to you? What do you mean to them?

Then ask yourself what each of these people want from the communication. Be sure you know the answers to this question.

- Cases 1, 2, and 3 at the end of Step 1 illustrate the People Questions.

These three People Questions are fundamental and apply across the board. Your answers will vary greatly according to circumstances, except that one answer to the first question is standard: Almost invariably you want results. You want your audience to act your way.

Your need to get results leads to Step 2.

Step 2   Use Motivators

This step has two guides:
- Catch and hold their attention.
- Show them the why.

Step 2 deals with a basic truth of human relations. You and I act the way we do because we are motivated to act that way — we want to act that way. Step 2 does not explore motivation in detail, but, rather, shows where it fits into a system for successful management communications and reviews key principles for motivating people to work effectively.

The first guide — Catch and hold their attention — is obvious but often overlooked. Before you can motivate me to do anything, you must catch and hold my attention. If I am not paying attention to you, then you aren't getting your message across to me—so how can you possibly motivate me?

Too many of the written and oral communications of business ignore this first guide. Deadly dull, badly structured, wordy, pompous reports and instructions seldom catch and hold anyone's attention. The authors of these communications are also ignoring the third People Question—What do they want? Busy managers do not want to read or listen to long, dull reports, nor do they want to wade through pages of tedious directives. Unfortunately in some large organizations, this disease of paper work proliferation is rapidly spreading.

The second guide—Show them the why—stresses the need to motivate your audience to act your way, or, more correctly, to show them the motivators which will help them decide to act your way. These motivators are the benefits (direct or indirect, negative or positive, individual or organizational) which should accrue to them from so acting.

- Case 4, following the second guide, illustrates the use of motivators.
- At the end of Step 2, motivation is considered in more detail under two headings—sales motivators and job motivators. Discussed under job motivators is the application of Maslow's hierarchy of needs, and McGregor's Theory X and Theory Y, to successful management communications.

STRUCTURE

This second blue chip heading of the Behind the Words system collects the key steps and guides concerning the planning and organizing necessary for successful management communications.

Every successful message has a structure—the successful business message usually has a tight, clear structure. To develop such a structure, build a poker chip outline.

Step 3   Build a Poker Chip Outline

This step has three guides:
- Identify your poker chips.
- Arrange in appropriate sequence.
- Decide your opening and closing.

To identify your poker chips, identify first your main ideas, or blue chips; then identify the subordinate, or red chip, ideas that belong under each blue chip, and, if appropriate, the white chip ideas that belong under each red chip.

For convenience, consider the opening of your message as your first blue chip and the closing as your last blue chip, even though each may be shorter in length than the blue chips constituting the body of your message and even though the opening and closing may stand apart from the body of the message. If you have an opening or closing at a subordinate level, again consider either as a part of the poker chips constituting that level.

To arrange your poker chips in appropriate sequence after you have identified them, first arrange the blue chips in the sequence you want to present them; then continue by arranging the red chips and white chips in the appropriate sequences for each. Possible sequences include point first, point last, straight line, and rambling.

To decide your opening and closing, review the People Steps and the poker chip outline you have built up to this point. Select an opening that establishes contact; previews the subject; and summarizes key facts, findings, and recommendations. The closing you choose, if any, depends greatly on the type of message.

The concept of a poker chip outline applies across the board, to writing, speaking, reading, or listening. Use it when

you are organizing your own message or when you are seeking the structure in someone else's message.

- Cases 5, 6, 7, and 8 at the end of Step 3 illustrate the
  guides in this step.

Step 4   Plan a Visible Structure

This step has three white chip guides:
- Avoid continuous narrative;
- Show meaning through word order;
- Follow the Clear River Test.

In the two People Steps and in the first Structure Step, the
emphasis is on concepts and the structure of ideas. In this
Step 4, the emphasis shifts to the structure of sentences and
paragraphs. The three guides will help you to plan a visible
structure for your message, so that your message will be
clearer to your audience. Although these guides apply primarily to the written word, the first three guides are also
useful in oral presentations or face-to-face communications.
A summary of the guides follows:

Avoid continous narrative. Leave this to the novelist; it is
seldom appropriate for business writing (or speaking). Use
signposts freely. Plan a readable layout.
Show meaning through word order. Discard the bugaboos
of traditional grammar; order is the key to the English
sentence. (Included here is a discussion of the erroneous
assumptions underlying every English grammar for 150
years and the change in approach reflected in the newer
dictionaries.)
Follow the Clear River Test. Use this simple readability
test to avoid creating unnecessary obstacles to readability.

At the end of Step 4 is a discussion of the IF-THEN structure of rules (statutes, regulations, directives, orders, manuals, instructions, etc.), including the use of decision tables
to chart this structure.

ACTION

The final blue chip heading of the Behind the Words system collects the key steps and guides concerning the act of communicating.

Step 5   Follow the BRISLEDITCH Guides

The basic principles for using words well, whether writing or speaking, may be conveniently grouped under these five guides:

- *Be brief*—Cut out useless words.
- *Be simple*—Avoid gobbledygook and pompous polysyllables.
- *Be direct*—Use strong, active verbs and normal sentence order.
- *Be clear*—Be sure your audience understands your words.
- *Be human*—People communicate with people.

The underlined letters spell the acronym BRISLEDITCH (pronounce it "Bristle Ditch").

There is no magic about this list of five, but they do help remind us of most of the common problems relating to using words well. Each of these guides relates back to and applies one or more of the guides discussed under People or Structure.

Step 6   Write Effectively

This step concerns the act of writing itself and has three guides:

- *Dictate a rough draft from an outline.* This is the most efficient way to write your message (for reasons explained in this guide).
- *Scan your draft first.* Don't pick up your editorial pencil as soon as you start reading your own (or a subordinate's) draft; instead, scan it first for overall content and substance, applying the People Questions and looking for the use of motivators and for the poker chip outline.

- *Edit your draft vigorously.* Be as ruthless as time permits in editing your own words. Learn to view your words critically and skeptically. But, when reviewing a subordinate's writing, try to delegate editorial responsibility so as not to destroy his initiative.

Step 7   Read Effectively

This is a short step because most of the principles for effective reading (not to be confused with speed reading) have already been covered. Step 7 has three guides:
- Preread the message first.
- Choose your reading speed.
- Read for poker chip structure.

The first two guides emphasize the importance of selective reading at different speeds; the prereading process is comparable to, but much faster than, the process of scanning a draft described in Step 6. The last guide in Step 7 applies the Structure Steps to reading.

Step 8   Listen and Speak Effectively

This final step in the Behind the Words system combines listening and speaking because in face-to-face communications the two skills are closely related and interdependent. Effective listening is a vital skill in which few managers have had adequate training. Step 8 has five guides:
- *Chart progress on Purpose Vector.* Face-to-face communications are a fleeting thing. When the words are spoken, they are gone, unless recorded. If you later seek to analyze or review a meeting or conversation, to determine what went wrong (or right), this is difficult because you have no way to chart the intangibles of oral communications and thus of identifying the process by which speakers proceed toward their goals.

    The Purpose Vector offers a simple means of charting this process in face-to-face communications. It is so simple that with a little practice anyone can use it mentally (or with scratch paper) to help him see where a conversation is going and thus help him decide what to do or say next.

- *Use your spare listening time.* This is the key to effective listening. You can think several times faster than I can talk; you therefore have spare listening time while I talk. Do you use it to help you listen effectively, or do you allow your mind to wander off on unrelated excursions?

- *Listen for poker chip structure.* Use your spare time to listen for blue chips and red chips in the speaker's message.

- *Watch for and use nonverbal signals.* When you are listening, watch for the meaning conveyed by the speaker's nonverbal signals; when you are speaking, use nonverbal signals to reinforce your meaning.

- *Plan and rehearse the formal talk.* Use the People and Structure Steps to plan your talk; then rehearse it. Use visual aids to help get your points across.

THE BEHIND THE WORDS SYSTEM

Part 1
People

The first main blue chip heading of the Behind the Words system, and thus the first side of the Behind the Words triangle, is People. Under this heading are collected the key steps and guides concerning the human relations side of communicating. The People heading has two red chip steps:

Step 1   Ask the Three People Questions
Step 2   Use Motivators

Ask the Three People Questions

The three guides under Step 1 are worded as questions:

- What is your purpose?
- Who is involved?
- What do they want?

These three People Questions are first stated and explained; and then they are illustrated (at the end of Step 1) in Case 1 — The Friday Rush Job, Case 2 — No Job for Alice Green, and Case 3 — Advanced Green When Flashing.

WHAT IS YOUR PURPOSE?

If you don't know your purpose when you start to communicate, you are not likely to succeed. This is obvious but sometimes ignored. If you begin to talk or write before you have thought out your purpose, your message will probably show a lack of direction. If you begin to read or listen without stopping to consider why you are reading or listening, you risk either wasting your time or missing the message.

The first People Question — What is your purpose? — therefore asks you to stop and define your wants or purposes as you start the communications process. Perhaps your answer requires no more than a moment's reflection; perhaps it requires considerable thought. In either case, the time you take to answer this first question will be time well spent.

The answers to this question vary greatly from situation to situation. Only one generalization is useful — the sender of a business communication almost always want action or results. He is seldom communicating to entertain or even simply to inform. The results may be positive, specific action ("I will carry out your order," "I approve of this proposal") or it may be simply an acceptance ("I hear what you say and have no comments").

To answer the question — What is your purpose? — for a specific situation, divide your purposes into broad and specific categories, both for yourself and for your organization. Then be sure you answer the question for each of the four categories. Case 2 — No Job for Alice Green — illustrates the common failure of the sender of a message to define his purpose broadly.

This first question is worded from the point of view of the communicator, as he starts the communications process, whether speaking, reading, listening, or writing, or as he stops to analyze an unexpected obstacle in the communications process. As worded, the first question therefore asks you as communicator to look forward.

The first question is equally valuable, however, as a starting point in analyzing an unsatisfactory completed communication. In this case, a change of focus is helpful. Ask yourself the question as if you were the sender of the message, at the point in time at which the sender started to communicate. Decide what his apparent purpose was; then consider whether his communication failure started with a failure to properly define his purpose.

Case 1, at the end of this Step 1, shows the application of this question to the looking-forward situation; Cases 2 and 3 show its application in analyzing a completed message.

Deciding your purpose is also the first step in using the Purpose Vector presented in Step 8.

WHO IS INVOLVED?

The second People Question asks you to stop and consider all the other people involved in the communication.

People Communicate with People

People communicate with people; organizations do not communicate with organizations. Organizations cannot communicate; only the people inside them can communicate. (Formal corporate or official governmental action constitutes a limited exception to this statement.) Too often we see the impersonal communication, spoken or written as though the organization itself was doing the communicating and the people involved were immaterial; or the communication that fails from the beginning because the sender forgets that his audience consists of people, rather than numbers on a computer tape.

Name Them All

In answering this second People Question, name all the other people involved, either individually or as groups. For example, if you are writing a report, who else will read it beside the named addressees? If you are writing a sales letter, who else is likely to see it, both in your organization and in the customer's organization? If you are explaining a new policy to an associate, how soon will your conversation reach those who listen to the office grapevine, and what distortions will result when it does? Be sure to name all these people. If, on the other hand, you are reading or listening, be sure you know who the writer or speaker is.

Beware of the Negative Hidden Audience

Many of your written or spoken messages will have a secondary audience of people you did not address directly but who will receive your message indirectly. Sometimes these people constitute a negative hidden audience—they do not have the power to take affirmative action on your message, but they do have the power to block the action you desire.

The larger your organization, the more likely there are to be negative hidden audiences. Usually these are people who, though not in a direct reporting relationship upward or downward from you, will be affected by whatever action you propose. If they see a threat to themselves or their own particular area by your proposed action, then they become a negative hidden audience. To avoid this problem, bring this audience out in the open if you can; in any case, be sure to consider them fully first.

Consider Their Environment

Having named all the people in your audience, consider what you know about their environment. What is their educational background? What is their point of view and their training? What prejudices are they likely to have? Under what circumstances will they be receiving this message?

Suppose for example, you are personnel director of a division that includes research scientists, line managers and supervisors, key punch operators, and machinists in the shop. Your job is to explain a new vacation policy. Should you send a written memo to each of these people? Should you ask all of them to meet at one time, or separately according to their functions in the organization? Or should you write memos for each group? Would a written memo or a meeting be more effective?

If your thinking as to the various environments of these groups were to stop at this point, you at least would have recognized that each group has its own interests; for this vacation policy message, that breakdown might or might not be sufficient.

Sometimes you must go further, to avoid the obvious fallacy of assuming, for example, that all the research scientists will think alike, that all the repairmen will think alike, and that no repairman will think like a research scientist. It is helpful and necessary to divide your audience into groups in order to decide how to approach them, but often you must also remember that groups are made up of a separate, distinct, unique individuals. Family status and age of children, for example, might affect each employee's reaction to a new vacation policy far more than his educational level or position in the organization.

In considering environment, it sometimes helps to locate yourself and your various audiences within your and their organizational pyramids.

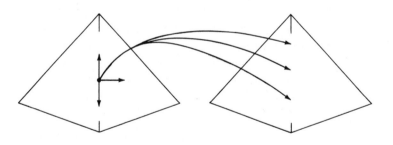

For example, the dot in the center of the left pyramid represents you, somewhere within the pyramid of your division in your organization. The right pyramid suggests the pyramid of another division in your organization or of another organization.

Where are your various audiences? Are they within your own pyramid, above, below, or next to you? Or are they in another pyramid, at the top, at the bottom, or in the middle? The arrows suggest the various possibilities.

In general, the farther away your audience is from you, functionally or geographically, the greater difficulty you will have communicating. Usually it is easy to communicate with an associate at the next desk but far less easy to communicate with someone you have never met who lives and works 1,000 miles away and whose job is substantially different from yours.

Remember also that each person is part of more than one pyramid. For example, if you are a manager in a division of your company 1,000 miles from corporate headquarters, you are inside the pyramid that represents your division; you are also inside the overall corporate pyramid. Your divisional pyramid may not necessarily fit neatly into the corporate pyramid. You also are inside separate and often overlapping pyramids representing your family; your community; and the civic, social, professional, or trade organizations of which you are a member.

The forces exerting pressure on you within each pyramid frequently pull you in opposite directions; the roles you play in each of these pyramids may vary widely. The table-pounding manager that terrifies his subordinates may submit mildly to his wife at home; he has worked off all his aggressions during the day. The lower-level manager who daily plods through a routine job may enter a new world of challenge or power as he leaves the office—perhaps as chairman of the local school board, leader of a boy scout troop, expert golfer or fisherman, or skilled cabinetmaker.

WHAT DO THEY WANT?

The third People Question requires you to ask yourself what each of these people want from the communication. Be sure you know the answers to this vital question.

Step in Their Shoes

To answer the question for each person or group in your audience, you must step in their shoes and look at the communication from their point of view and not from yours.

Step in their shoes. You can read those four words in a second or two, but how difficult it is for any of us to step into the shoes of another person. Yet, this is almost the basic key to success in human relations. When you have the insight, wisdom, and objectivity to turn around, step in the shoes of your audience, and look at a problem from their point of view and not from yours, then the information you gain can materially help you communicate effectively.

When you do this, be sure to think of each separate audience, as the wants of one audience are not necessarily the wants of others.

The first People Question asked you to consider both your specific and broad purposes, for yourself and for your organization. In answering this third People Question, consider the specific and broad wants of your various audiences, both as individuals and as members of an organization.

Meanings Are in People

In answering this third question, and in planning your message accordingly, remember that meanings of words are in people and not in dictionaries. Words seldom have fixed absolute meanings but, instead, meanings often change according to the user and the context. Furthermore, your understanding of the meaning of the words I use will almost surely not be precisely the same as mine, unless you and I are using our words carefully and understand each other well.

Suppose you listen to the president of a corporation conducting the annual meeting of stockholders; in the course of his remarks he makes a vigorous plea for retaining the "free enterprise" system in this country. Those words will have many meanings to his audience. To some, the connotations of free enterprise are admirable, desirable, and represent a cause to be fought for; to others, free enterprise is a nasty phrase, representing an outmoded system of rampant, uncontrolled capitalism. Others, a little more cautious and selective in their listening, may well think "what does he mean by 'free enterprise'?" Does he mean the free enterprise of sweatshops and child-labor factories in the 1850s? Does he mean the free enterprise of the pioneers who crossed the continents to open up new territories? Or does he simply mean that his company is facing new government controls which he intends to resist?

Meanings of words are also relative, depending on the time and place they are used. If I step out of my house on a January day after a week of below-freezing temperatures to find that the sun is out, the temperature is 40° F, and the snow is melting, I may say "It's warm outside"; but if I step outside of the same house in July after a week's heat wave to find a northwest wind has cooled the temperature to 70° F, I am likely to say "It's cool outside."

The point is to be sure you consider the possible unexpected meanings your audience may read into the words you use and therefore to explain yourself carefully to avoid misunderstanding. It is not enough to write or speak so that you will be understood; let your goal be to use words so carefully you cannot be misunderstood.

These three People Questions are fundamental and apply across the board to writing, speaking, reading, listening, or thinking. Let these questions become an automatic mental habit; ask yourself the questions before you start to write or speak. If you do, you will help yourself aim your communications in the right direction and you will avoid basic errors. Ask yourself the questions again, whenever your communications seem to be failing because of conflict or resistance from the receiver.

Because the answers to these questions vary greatly according to circumstances, no book could provide anyone with all possible answers. Our purpose here is to focus on the importance of asking ourselves these questions, even if for only a moment before we start the communications process. When we do, we greatly improve our chances of communicating successfully.

The following three cases illustrate the application of the People Questions.

CASE 1: THE FRIDAY RUSH JOB

You are at your desk on a Friday at 9 A.M. Your in-box contains an urgent request from Charlie Smith, vice-president, sales, that an important proposal be mailed today. Charlie says he promised the customer it would and adds that he will be out of town today. The proposal contains technical material that is being prepared in a department headed by one of your subordinates, Tom Cohen. You do not report to Charlie Smith, but your departments regularly provide the detailed technical information for sales proposals.

You call Tom Cohen into your office to pass the request along to him. To your surprise, Tom objects strenuously and presents several reasons why Charlie's request places an unreasonable burden on his department. Somewhat irritated and puzzled by Tom's unusual attitude, you press the matter further with him but avoid a direct order. His resistance continues.

At this point, what should have been a simple passing of an instruction from superior to subordinate has turned into an unexpected problem.

When your conversation with Tom started, you had subconsciously answered the People Questions according to a pattern that seemed reasonable to you. You wanted to comply with Charlie Smith's request to get the proposal out today.

This seemed a request Tom Cohen's people should be able to handle without serious problems. You didn't expect Tom to raise objections when you called him in, but now Tom's resistance has created a roadblock. To help analyze this roadblock, you should now mentally reexamine the People Questions in the light of this new situation.

What Is Your Purpose?—How hard are you prepared to push Tom to get this proposal out today?

Who Is Involved?—How important is this customer? How important is Charlie's goodwill to you? Does Charlie regularly make unreasonable demands? What about Tom? What is new about Tom at this moment that makes him resist you? Why is the Tom who sits before you at this moment not the same Tom that has sat before you on other occasions? Is he being unreasonable? Why? Are there problems at home that he is bringing to the office with him? Have you been so busy lately that you have not had time to look at him as a person? Or are his reasons for resisting this rush job valid and sensible ones based on the work load? Your mental analysis leads logically to the last People Question.

What Do They Want?—In this case, the "they" includes Charlie, Tom, and the customer. How important is it to get this proposal out? What is behind Tom's resistance? What does Charlie really want?

Note that the answers to the People Questions are closely interrelated and overlapping in this case. This often happens.

The answers to all these questions involve knowing many facts not presented here. The purpose of this case is not to present a final solution, but rather to show how the People Questions can help you communicate effectively when a roadblock unexpectedly develops in face-to-face communications.

Let's assume your quick mental review of the People Questions at this point suggested to you that you should pause before ordering Tom to do the job.

So therefore you did stop to talk with Tom for a few

minutes. You could have ordered Tom to get the work done, and he would have done it. But, if you had, you realized you might never get answers to some important questions concerning your relationship with Tom.

Let's assume further that, as a result of this conversation, you found, first, that Tom was disgruntled because you had been too busy recently to talk to him, and second, that he had valid reasons for believing that Charlie's request not only was unreasonable but would be difficult to comply with without pushing other equally important jobs aside. You therefore decided not to order Tom to get the rush job out today, if it would seriously disrupt other important work.

Your thoughts next turn to the customer. Do you notify him of the delay today, and, if so, by phone or by letter? Or do you wait for Charlie to return on Monday? You have spoken to Charlie's assistant but he refuses to take any responsibility.

Again, you use the People Questions to help you analyze the pros and cons of these three alternatives.

What is your purpose? Having decided that the proposal need not go out today, you now want to keep the customer and Charlie as happy as possible. *Who is involved?* How well do you know the customer? Are you on a first-name basis so that you can pick up the phone and explain the problem (at the same time being prepared to yield and give the proposal top priority if someone in the customer's office insists)? Or is the customer a stranger to you so that the results of a phone call are unpredictable? Finally, *What do they want?* "They" now means Charlie and the customer. Would Charlie resent your contacting the customer yourself, or would he prefer to have you settle the matter?

All of us are familiar with this kind of unexpected resistance in our day-to-day relations with our superiors, subordinates, and associates (and also our family and friends). The person we are talking to does not react the way we expected. What is wrong? When these situations arise in face-to-face communications, mentally apply the People Questions to the new situation. Use these questions as a mental checklist and a means of developing the answers that will help you most effectively get around the roadblock that has suddenly appeared.

CASE 2: NO JOB FOR ALICE GREEN

Alice Green was graduating from high school in June. Late one April afternoon, she applied for a job at the local bank. Mary Rush, the employment interviewer, asked Alice to complete an application, gave her a shorthand and typing test, and then talked to her for a few minutes, explaining that it was too late in the day for further interviews. A week later, Alice Green received this letter:

Dear Miss Green:

We have completed our review of your recent application and test results. We find we are unable to offer a position to you at this time.

> Very truly yours,
> M. C. Rush
> Personnel Department

When Alice received this curt letter, she felt as if a bucket of cold water had been dumped on her head. This was the first job she applied for; she had thought she would qualify; and Miss Rush had said nothing to her to suggest that she would not. Feeling discouraged, she showed the letter to her parents, to the guidance counselor at school, and to her close friends.

- This letter, used regularly by an employment interviewer of a moderate-sized bank for several years, wins no prizes for friendliness, tact, or even a minimum of ordinary business courtesy.

■ It is a splendid example of the kind of letter where the writer seems to have forgotten entirely that people communicate with people. Even though Mary Rush was only a few years older than Alice Green, she apparently had no ability to step in Alice's shoes and consider how Alice would react to this entire situation.

The story did not end here, however. The guidance counselor called Mary Rush to ask for more facts as to why Alice was turned down; Alice's father, a customer of the bank for twenty years, sent the letter to the president, with the suggestion that there must have been a better way of handling the situation; and the president sent the letter to the personnel vice-president with the comment "Is this necessary?"

If we use the People Questions to analyze this letter and the underlying situation, we find that these questions provide an orderly means of pinpointing several problems.

What is your purpose? In this letter, Mary Rush clearly wanted to tell Alice that there was no job for her at this time. She succeeded in doing that admirably and thus apparently accomplished her own specific objective of closing out the case, and the bank's specific objective of saying no to the applicant. But she completely overlooked the broader objectives, for both herself and the bank. A letter such as this, lacking in simple business courtesy, unnecessarily antagonizes its audience or, at the least, reflects unfavorably on the writer and his organization.

Who is involved? This is where the letter really fell down. Mary Rush, wearing blinders when she wrote this letter, was thinking only of an eighteen-year old high school graduate and not of the probable larger audience for this letter. In fact, this audience included the girl's parents who were customers of the bank; the guidance counselor at school, who would decide whether to recommend to other seniors that they apply for jobs at this bank; the girl's friends, who were both potential job applicants and potential bank customers; and the president and personnel vice-president of the bank.

Thus a negative hidden audience clearly existed here that Mary Rush entirely ignored.

What do they want? In this case, the answers to the first two questions largely provide the answers to this third question. First, Alice Green, her parents, the guidance counselor, and perhaps her friends would have liked an explanation as to why she was turned down. This information was not included in the letter. Second, all these people would have reacted favorably to simple business courtesy.

For example, the following minimum changes would have made this letter more acceptable although the explanation of why Alice was turned down is still lacking:

Dear Alice:

Thank you for applying for a job at our bank.

We have carefully reviewed your application. I am sorry to tell you we cannot offer you a position now.

> Sincerely,
> Mary C. Rush
> Employment Interviewer

This letter is introduced as Case 2 because the problems it presents are highlighted when the People Questions are applied to the letter. It is too short to present structure problems; the failure to motivate, although present, is better illustrated by other examples.

The People Questions are also used to help analyze other cases and examples of poor communications in this book, but where communications are more complex, the questions become simply a starting point.

The next case illustrates another communications failure where the People Questions help highlight the problem.

CASE 3: ADVANCED GREEN WHEN FLASHING

In Toronto, Ottawa, and other cities in Ontario, a traffic sign reading "Advanced Green When Flashing" appears underneath many traffic lights at major intersections.

To motorists familiar with the traffic-light pattern in use in these cities, the sign conveys a definite and clear meaning.

But how clear are these four words to a stranger from the States who reads this sign for the first time as he approaches a busy intersection and finds the green light flashing? The answer must be that these words convey no information because, by themselves, they are meaningless to a stranger.

The sign is intended to tell the motorist that the green light will flash for a few seconds at the beginning of the green cycle. During this flashing cycle, he may safely turn left because the light remains red for traffic coming the other way. A flashing green light is therefore similar to a combination of a solid green light and a green arrow pointing left, and is much safer than the practice in many United States cities of advancing the green light on one side without in any way indicating this to the motorist.

Let's apply the three People Questions to this sign.

What is your purpose? The traffic engineer's purpose should have been to design a sign that communicated quickly, simply, and clearly to any motorist the necessary information regarding the traffic-light cycle.

Who is involved? This is the key question here. The engineer was thinking only of an audience who already knew the traffic-light pattern and thus already knew what the four words meant. Such an audience might include fellow traffic engineers or residents of the city where the sign appeared.

He ignored the fact that the broader audience of motorists, from the States or from outside Ontario, who see the sign for the first time are not familiar with the light cycle. He overlooked the safety hazard caused by such motorists stopping or slowing down to puzzle at the sign's meaning.

But this traffic engineer was no worse than many of his fellow engineers in the United States. Almost every interstate highway has examples of poorly worded signs, puzzling and confusing to the stranger. He was no worse, also, than many other managers, professionals, and technical people who fail to consider the broader audience for their instructions or reports. It is easy to communicate with your associate at the next desk; you speak the same technical language and in-house jargon he does, and you know him personally. It is easy to design a traffic sign intelligible to someone who already knows the traffic pattern and the city and needs only a reminder.

What do they want? The third question helps us complete the analysis.

Motorists, particularly strangers, want traffic instructions that can be read and understood quickly. "Advanced Green When Flashing" can be read quickly but is meaningless to a stranger.

Use Motivators

The first People Question asks What is your purpose? For business communications, one general answer is that you want results from your communications. You are communicating with me because you want me to act your way.

Stated in the most basic terms, I act in a particular way because I see more benefits to be gained by acting than by not acting. The benefits may be negative (freedom from fear, freedom from pain); they may be emotional (I want power, happiness, success, recognition); they may be rational (if I buy this machine, it will save us money).

To motivate me to act your way you must first understand me and my wants (the second and third People Questions), and then you must communicate to me or create in my environment those reasons or facts (often called "motivators") which I can accept as a part of my motives for acting your way.

How do you get results? How do you motivate me to act your way? The word "motivate" means to provide with a motive. (But it is important to note that "motivate" does not mean "manipulate.") In deciding whether to act your way I may, exercising my own free will, accept or reject any or all of the motives you suggest to me. Accordingly, I may decide to act your way because of or in spite of the motives you suggest; I may decide not to act your way because or in spite of the motives you suggest; or I may find entirely different motives for acting your way.

Only I can decide which motives I accept or am influenced by in deciding to act in a particular way. A motive is an emotion, idea, need, or want arising within me which leads me to action. Perhaps you motivated me by providing me with a reason which I accepted as my motive; perhaps I provided it myself; more likely, both happened.

Motivation is a large subject; the purpose of this Step 2 is to identify motivation as one of the eight basic steps in the Behind the Words system and to summarize the principles for motivating, at two levels. These are:

- Catch and hold attention

    At this first level, your job as sender of a message is to motivate me, as your audience, to read or listen to the message. If I am not paying attention to you, then how can you expect me to act your way?

- Show them the why

    This guide concerns the content of the message. If you want me to act your way, show me the benefits I can expect to gain from so acting. Don't merely recite the facts; also state the benefits. Answer my basic questions: "What's in this for me?" "Why should I act your way?"

CATCH AND HOLD THEIR ATTENTION

The first guide is an essential preliminary to motivating anyone to do anything. If you do not catch and hold your audience's attention, then they obviously will not receive your message as you intended. Too many business communications ignore this first principle. Dull, wordy, poorly structured, and pompous reports, letters, memos, speeches, and instructions seldom catch and hold anyone's attention. Too often they gather dust on a desk until they are filed away half-read and half-understood.

Paper Work Proliferation

The larger the organization, the greater the problem here. Paper work proliferation is a deadly disease in most large organizations, public or private.

The small- or medium-sized organization rarely suffers from severe paper work proliferation. Work gets done without elaborate systems of written reports and countless written instructions.

Some of the added paper work of the large organization is unavoidable, but much of it can be avoided. More written reports and instructions are necessary in the larger organization because more people in more locations must be kept informed. Also, management needs written reports to effectively control the work of the organization because face-to-face contact is impossible between so many people. To that extent, the larger volume of written reports and instructions in the large organization is acceptable. Beyond that, it is not acceptable.

For example, a serious problem of paper work proliferation exists in a large federal agency whose directives system appears to be slowly collapsing under its own weight. Directives in this system tend to be written in a wordy, rambling, polysyllabic, continuous narrative style. As is true in many agencies, the basic directive on a particular matter, issued at the department level, is in almost every case supplemented by further directives at the bureau and field level; but generally each level repeats in part and paraphrases in part the higher-level directives. The various directives occupy many volumes; new directives are published almost daily.

The unfortunate user often must struggle through three levels of directives on the same subject to find what he should do.

Yet this level-by-level structure and continuous narrative style apparently developed from the best intentions. Headquarters did not want to stifle initiative by issuing precise detailed regulations on every point, so the directive at the highest level was intended to set forth broad policy, and in turn each lower level implemented this policy with a more detailed directive. The continuous narrative style was felt to be appropriate because it avoided a peremptory military style of order.

Perhaps these reasons were sound when the system was first started some years ago, but unfortunately the result is paper work proliferation of the worst sort. (As to the disadvantages, in a directive or instruction, of continuous narrative and the advantages of a step-by-step listing which avoids the peremptory style, see Step 4—Plan a Visible Structure.)

In practice, many users of this directives system no longer read the directives when they want a reliable answer to a new question. Instead, they pick up the phone and talk to the specialist in the subject-matter area. (The specialist is delighted to be asked. The more inquiries he receives, the more important his job.) Thus, they take the right action but, in so doing, certainly raise basic questions—why have a directives system if people have given up using it to answer difficult questions; and, how much time and money is wasted because managers phone the specialist rather than looking the answer up in the book?

A further problem appears when it becomes necessary to call everyone's attention to an important new directive. People realize that something more is required than simply publishing the directive, because they are aware that addressees may or may not read it carefully. Sometimes, therefore, there has to be a memo warning people to be sure to read the important new directive; and sometimes staff meetings must also be held to tell people to read it (and of course memos and directives must be issued on the need to hold staff meetings). After a while, the wheels begin to spin.

Captive Audience Fallacy

Paper work proliferation is sometimes caused because the sender of a written message is guilty of the fallacy of assuming that he has a captive audience. Because I write a report to you and send copies of it to six other people, does this mean that each of these people will read my report carefully and thoughtfully from beginning to end the moment it arrives in their in-box? Of course not, unless my report is of unusual importance or unless I am the president of the company. My report is competing for attention with everything else on each person's desk and in each person's mind from the moment that he takes it from his in-box to look at it.

Consider the process as it applies to you when you are reading the mail in your in-box. What choices do you have as you look at each item, and what is the process which you follow? Do you read each item through carefully and thoughtfully from beginning to end and then stop and act on it? Probably not; probably instead you preread each item quickly to discover in general what it is all about; and then, depending on what you find, decide to:

1. act on it immediately or as soon as you can;
2. put it aside, for further consideration later, on that slow pile that gathers dust at the back of your desk;
3. check your initials and flip it into the out-box, half-read and half-understood, for someone else to act on; or
4. quietly drop it in the wastebasket.

What makes you decide that a particular item will get treatment 1 instead of treatment 4? At least two factors could affect your decision. First, the item looks important; and, second, it looks as though you can read it, understand it, and act on it without too much difficulty. We all tend to put aside for later consideration or pass on to someone else messages that look difficult or look as though they would require much more time.

If you want me to act promptly on your written message, you must therefore catch and hold my attention. After I pick your message out of my in-box, no matter how skillful and how effective you are in finding and suggesting to me the motivators which will persuade me to act your way, nothing is accomplished until you have caught and held my attention and motivated me to take the first step, namely, to read the message.

The need to catch and hold attention is also vital in one-way oral communication. If I am making a formal presentation or speech to a group, obviously I must catch and hold their attention from my very first words. If I don't, I have lost my audience and I will not get the results I seek. We have all heard speakers, whether in an informal business meeting or from a podium, who failed to catch and hold our attention.

The situation is somewhat different in face-to-face communications, because here the listener can ask questions, make comments, or interrupt. Thus, the speaker has the benefit of feedback and, if he is at all observant, can detect whether his message is getting across.

How do you catch and hold attention? The answers to this vary widely with the type of communication and the situation in which it occurs. There are two valid generalizations, however. To catch and hold my attention, (1) you must show me from the beginning that your message is important to me, and (2) you must present to me a clear, simple, well-structured message, so that I do not become lost, bewildered, or bored.

SHOW THEM THE WHY

Having motivated me to listen to your message, your next step is to motivate me to take the action that you want me to take, or more correctly, to show me the motivators which will help me decide to act your way. Case 4, which follows, illustrates the use of motivators in four situations — making a sale, reporting to a superior, reassuring an associate, instructing and counseling subordinates. Following Case 4 is a discussion of motivation in selling and managing, including the application of Maslow's hierarchy of needs, and McGregor's Theory X and Theory Y, to successful management communications.

CASE 4: THE BACKLOG IN CUSTOMER SERVICE

The Problem

Helen Watkins is the newly appointed director of Customer Service at the Central Co., a moderate-sized business with customers throughout the country. One of Helen's departments handles customer correspondence; its job is to answer customer inquiries and complaints. When Helen started her new job a month ago, Customer Service had a one month's backlog of customer letters. Some customers were writing a second letter, often to the president of Central Co., Walter King, before the first had been answered. Because of the pressure to clean up the backlog, correspondents were more concerned with quantity than quality, so that many letters were poorly written, tactless, and simply did not answer the customer's question.

Walter King's instructions to Helen were to the point: "Helen, I want that backlog cleaned up, and I want our customers to get prompt, complete, and courteous answers to their letters. Use your own best judgment; report back to me within a month with your plan."

When Helen studied the correspondence operation, she found the following:

1. The backlog was becoming worse rather than better. Therefore prompt and vigorous action would be required.

2. Less-experienced correspondents received batches of twenty routine letters with necessary files attached. Their job was to read the letter, study the file, do any necessary research, and then answer the letter. Forty letters per day per correspondent was considered a reasonable quota.

3. The more experienced correspondents received batches of ten more complex letters, but otherwise followed the same procedure. Their quota, although more flexible, was understood to be twenty per day per correspondent.

4. The correspondent wrote the answer in longhand, often referring by number to standard paragraphs in a manual. No dictating equipment was available. Helen noted that the standard paragraphs were not always appropriate, but correspondents found it easier to use the standard paragraph than to write a more appropriate paragraph by hand.

5. A unit supervisor reviewed each letter and signed it with Helen's name. Because of the backlog, the review process was perfunctory.

6. Because of the batching system, there was no continuity. If the customer wrote a second letter, it would probably be routed to a different correspondent.

7. Unit supervisors were permitted, but not encouraged, to phone customers whose problems were unusually complex. Correspondents seldom phoned a customer.

8. Morale in the section was poor and turnover was high.

9. Helen's random sampling of outgoing letters quickly

convinced her that too many letters were poorly written
and curt and did not answer the customer's questions.

10. There was no formal training program because of the
pressure of work. New correspondents learned by trial
and error, because unit supervisors were too busy to
provide effective training.

The Solution

After completing her review, Helen asked a business machine
company to review the operation and tell her the advantages,
if any, of providing dictating machines for each correspondent
and automatic typewriters and transcribers for each typist.

The salesman did a thorough job. After studying the operation, he prepared a written proposal to Helen and presented
it to her orally. He opened his presentation by showing Helen
a simple chart summarizing time savings. To develop these
figures, he determined the average overall output of the
section per week in typewriter lines, and then applied factors
for the time saved by the correspondent in using dictating
equipment and by the typist in using automatic typewriters.
The salesman estimated that the equipment would pay for
itself in three years, that it would increase productivity by
50 percent, and that the backlog could be eliminated in six
months.

Next, Helen looked at the job itself. She found that correspondents handling the routine letters were bored and frustrated, disliked the high quotas, resented having all letters
reviewed and signed by the unit supervisor in a third person's
name, and felt they were little more than automatons. The
more conscientious correspondents knew that they could
not possibly do a satisfactory job under the circumstances.
Furthermore, a correspondent felt little responsibility for his
answer. If it was not satisfactory, he would never know it
because the next letter would go to another correspondent.

Thus, Helen realized, the correspondents were not motivated to do their jobs well. She decided to change this by giving each correspondent a fair mix of the routine and the more complex letters; by allowing each correspondent to sign each letter with his own name; by eliminating the review of each letter and substituting instead a quality control based on random sampling; by deemphasizing rigid quota requirements and instead emphasizing the importance of the correct answer the first time; by encouraging the use of the phone; and by training correspondents through workshops in effective communications.

Helen's next concern was the sales vice-president. How would he react to the greatly increased use of the phone by the correspondents? Would he see Helen as an empire builder, whose proposal would encroach on the salesmen's job? Would he feel that only salesmen should be allowed to talk to customers?

In short, was the sales vice-president a potential negative hidden audience who could kill Helen's proposal?

To avoid any problems, Helen met with the sales vice-president. She pointed out that better customer service would relieve salesmen of the chore of handling profitless service problems, that correspondents would be trained in the use of the phone, and that a higher customer retention rate would make the sales department's record look better. The vice-president seemed satisfied.

Before going ahead, Helen knew that she had to report to the president and obtain his approval. She therefore prepared a written report and made an oral presentation to the president. She rehearsed her presentation in advance, so that she could summarize her key points in two minutes. These key points, identical with those appearing in the one-page summary of her report, were as follows: the backlog could be cleaned up within three months after the new equipment was installed and correspondents and typists trained to use it;

thereafter the section could remain current, except for seasonal peaks; no new employees would need to be hired; the quality of the letters would materially improve because of the upgrading of the job. The only alternative was to hire several more employees, but this would require additional work space which was not available; and, more important, the cost would be greater than the method Helen proposed.

The president approved Helen's recommendations and complimented her on her well-organized and brief presentation. Helen ordered the equipment and proceeded with the other steps in the plan, including holding a meeting for all the correspondents at which she outlined the changes that would be made.

Six months later, the backlog was in fact cleaned up and the new equipment and the new manuals were in effect.

The Motivators for Each Communication

There were at least five key communications situations in this case. In each of these, the sender of the communication effectively found and suggested to the receiver of the communication appropriate motivators. Let's look at these five:

1. The president motivated Helen by presenting her with a challenge and giving her a free hand, subject to the requirement that she report back. Helen recognized that if she solved the backlog problem, the president would be favorably impressed and her career would be materially helped. Likewise, if she failed to solve it, her career would be set back. In presenting Helen with a challenge and in giving her the freedom to develop her own plan, the president was using two powerful job motivators—the opportunity to achieve success, and freedom on the job. The president was a Theory Y manager at this point. (See "Job Motivators" p. 53.)

   But, like any good manager, the president did not delegate completely to Helen the task of solving the backlog problem. He required Helen to report back within a month. Thus, behind the participative Theory Y delegation to Helen remained an unspoken, latent Theory X requirement that Helen's solution be ready within a month and that it work. The president here was using the ultimate Theory X motivator of fear—in this case, fear of failure.

2. The salesman motivated Helen to purchase the dictating equipment and automatic typewriters because he studied the needs of the correspondence section carefully and prepared a proposal that showed the time savings if she purchased the equipment. Thus, the backlog could be eliminated in six months.

   The salesman was therefore motivating Helen to buy by showing her the tangible benefits of purchasing the equipment—eliminating the backlog and saving time in the future.

3. When Helen met with the correspondents and explained to them the changes she proposed in their job, she was motivating them to work more effectively because she was offering them a more interesting job with greater challenge, greater responsibility, and more freedom. (This motivational approach to the job itself is usually called "job enrichment".)

4. Because Helen took the time to show the sales vice-president how her proposal would benefit, and could not harm, the sales department, she won the sales vice-president's approval and eliminated a possible negative audience.

5. When Helen reported to the president and proposed her solutions, she won the president's quick approval, not only because her proposal was sound, but also because she knew that the president was busy and thus she had carefully prepared her two-minute summary presentation.

MOTIVATION IN SELLING AND MANAGING

In answering the second People Question—Who is involved?
—we saw that it often helps to place yourself and your
audience within and their respective organizational
pyramids. The two pyramids below locate the people discussed in Case 4:

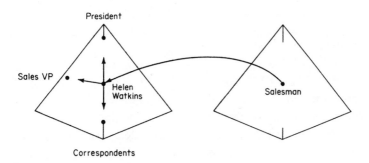

The types of motivators frequently depend on the direction
of the arrows, although every motivator relies on the basic
principle stated as the title of this guide—Show them the why.
If you want me to act your way, show me the benefits I can
expect to gain from so acting; answer for me the basic question, "What's in it for me?"

A useful classification of motivators is into two types—
those used in selling or proposing (sales motivators) and
those used in managing subordinates (job motivators). For
the job motivators, the arrow goes down on the pyramid from
us to our subordinates. For the sales motivators, the arrow
goes across or up from us to our associates or superiors within
the pyramid, or outside the pyramid to our prospects, customers, or the public.

Sales Motivators

In Case 4, the salesman showed Helen why she should buy

the dictating equipment and automatic typewriters by showing her how these would solve the backlog problem at a reasonable cost. The salesman thus answered Helen's unspoken question, "Why should I buy your equipment?" by in effect saying, "If you buy my equipment, both you and your department will benefit because it will solve your backlog problems at a reasonable cost, and this in turn will impress the president with your competence." Perhaps the salesman, in talking to Helen, suggested the second motive of impressing the president; more likely he didn't need to because he sensed that Helen was already aware of it.

The point here is that the salesman did not simply recite the facts about his product, but rather he studied Helen's problem and showed her the benefits she could expect from buying this equipment.

Helen answered the sales vice-president's unspoken question, "Why should I go along with your solution to the backlog problem?" by in effect saying, "If you go along with my solution, your salesmen will answer less service calls and your customer retention percentages should improve. This will improve the performance of your department."

Again, Helen did not simply tell the vice-president the facts of the new equipment, but she took the trouble to explain how this new equipment would help the vice-president.

Helen answered the president's unspoken question, "Why should I agree to your proposal?" by in effect saying, "If you agree to my proposal, you and your company will benefit because it will solve the backlog problem, increase customer retention, and reduce customer complaints. This will solve a persistent problem that has been taking too much of your time."

The three simple examples above could be multiplied many times over, but the principle would remain the same. Whether you are a salesman talking to a prospect, a manager proposing a new program to a superior or explaining the program to an associate, you are selling. To motivate the buyer, whether he be a customer, superior, or associate, don't stop with the facts of your proposal, but show him the why—tell him why your proposal will benefit him and his organization. Don't assume that he will see the benefits without being told; state them clearly. Sometimes these benefits are direct, tangible, and clearly identified in terms of dollars or time saved. In other cases, they are highly intangible personal considerations of gain, prestige, status, etc.

These sales motivators belong here in the process of communications because, before you structure your message, you must know what motivators, if any, you will use as a part of that structure.

This is not a book on the sales process; the above is intended rather as a brief review of an important principle for successful communications.

Job Motivators

The job motivators are illustrated in this case, first, by the president's communication to Helen when he offered her the opportunity to achieve and gave her freedom on the job in investigating the problem, and, second, by Helen's restructuring of the correspondents' job to give them greater freedom on the job and thus in turn a greater feeling of achievement, challenge, and satisfaction.

It is appropriate at this point to review briefly current theory on managing and motivating subordinates. McGregor's Theory X and Theory Y serves as a useful framework for this review.[1]

McGregor calls Theory X the traditional view of direction and control and sums it up as being based on the assumption that people inherently dislike work and will avoid it if they can. Most people must therefore be coerced, controlled,

[1] McGregor, Douglas, *The Human Side of Enterprise*, New York: McGraw-Hill Book Company, 1960.

directed, and threatened with punishment to get them to work adequately toward achieving organizational objectives. Furthermore, most people prefer to be directed, wish to avoid responsibility, have relatively little ambition, and want security above all.

Theory Y allows individual and organizational goals to be integrated and assumes that the dreary precepts of Theory X are false. Theory Y says that controls and threats of punishment are not the only way to make people work toward organizational objectives. People are not inherently lazy and will exercise self-direction and self-control towards objectives to which they are committed. This commitment is a function of the rewards associated with achievement of the objectives.

People will learn under proper conditions, Theory Y holds, not only to accept but to seek responsibility. The capacity to exercise imagination, ingenuity, and creativity in the solution of organizational problems is widely, not narrowly, distributed in the population; but unfortunately most people at work use only a small proportion of their intellectual potential.

Theory X and Theory Y are built on Maslow's hierarchy of needs.[2] In contrasting Theory X and Theory Y, McGregor explains this hierarchy as follows: Man is a wanting animal, Maslow said. As soon as one of his needs is satisfied, another appears in its place. This unending process means that human needs are organized in a series of levels — a hierarchy of importance. A satisfied need at a lower level is no longer a motivator of behavior. This fact of profound significance is ignored by Theory X but recognized by Theory Y.

The hierarchy of needs starts at the lowest level with the basic or physiological needs, such as food, rest, shelter, protection.

When these basic needs are reasonably satisfied, the safety

[2] See A. H. Maslow, *Motivation and Personality.* New York: Harper & Brothers, 1954.

needs begin to dominate man's behavior. These include protection against danger, threat, deprivation.

When man's basic and safety needs are satisfied, his social
needs become important motivators of his behavior. These
include the need for belonging, for acceptance, for giving and
receiving friendship and love.

Above the social needs, come the ego needs. These are of
two kinds: — those relating to each man's opinion of himself —
the need for self-respect, self-confidence, autonomy, achievement, competence, and knowledge; and those relating to what
other people think of him (his reputation) — including status,
recognition, appreciation, and deserved respect.

At the top of the hierarchy are the need for self-fulfillment,
including the realizing of one's own full potential; the need for
continued self-development; and the need for being creative in
the broadest sense of that term. These top needs, like the ego
needs, are never fully satisfied.

Most employees today find their basic and safety needs
satisfied and therefore seek to satisfy their social, ego, and
self-fulfillment needs. A Theory X management philosophy
does nothing to satisfy any of these higher needs. Theory Y,
by integrating individual and organization goals, does offer
the employee the opportunity to satisfy these higher needs.

The thinking behind McGregor's Theory X and Theory Y
has been refined and expanded by others, but his basic theory
still remains a convenient and dramatic way of contrasting
the traditional view of direction and control with an approach
that takes into consideration the hierarchy of needs.

Where did Theory X, as the traditional view of direction and
control, originate? Why did this autocratic philosophy of
management become the standard when large organizations,
corporate and government, first made their appearance in
the nineteenth century? The answer is that the only existing
organizations of any size at that time were the Army and the

Roman Catholic Church. Both of these were built on a rigid, autocratic Theory X–type hierarchy, requiring unquestioned obedience. The punishment for disobedience was court-martial or excommunication.

Today, the church can no longer effectively enforce its edicts by the threat of excommunication; and the Army finds that the threat of court-martial no longer has the sting it formerly had.

The same is even truer in the business organization. The absolute power to fire an employee without cause because he displeases the boss still exists but in nothing like the degree that it was found one hundred years ago. Unions protect their members; the Civil Service Commission and the law protect government employees; enlightened personnel policies save many other employees from arbitrary action; and at the same time, increased or transferable pension, health, social security and unemployment benefits make the firing process a little less unpleasant for the employee.

Simultaneously, our entire society is moving away from an autocratic model to a more participative one. Fathers no longer dominate family units as autocrats; faculties no longer demand of students lockstep learning by rote and enforce rigid discipline for any failure; throughout our society the power of authority everywhere is losing its hold. One important reason for this is the need in our increasingly complex society for interdependence. Few of us today are either wholly dependent upon others or wholly independent of others. The slave on a cotton plantation and the worker in an early nineteenth century sweatshop were each wholly dependent on his employer; the pioneers crossing the continent to find new frontiers were dependent on no one but themselves. But today's society is so complex that interdependence is the norm.

To the extent therefore that today's managers are somewhat more Theory Y–oriented than were their fathers, this may reflect a concurrent change away from authority in the attitude of society. If this is so, and it seems unavoidably so, then the autocratic hierarchal organization patterned after the Army and the Roman Catholic Church, and typical of almost every corporation or government bureaucracy, may well be already obsolete; but we have found no substitute, because as a manager climbs the ladder, one of his strong ego needs becomes the need for power.

McGregor and Maslow label the need for achievement a key ego need but, unfortunately, "achievement" may be too gentle a term in some cases. The real force that drives and inspires many managers to climb up and up is the need for power and the satisfaction of exercising power. A manager who is strongly motivated by this drive is not likely to be a true Theory Y manager, no matter how much lip service he may pay to the concept. Herein lies the basic problem and the reason why we are unlikely to see any immediate change in the autocratic structure of organizations.

- The newly appointed president of a large bank was asked how it felt to be at the top. He thought for a few moments of the fifteen years he had spent fighting his way up the corporate ladder, and, in particular, of his last four years as executive vice-president under a president who was a demanding perfectionist. His answer was, "Now it's my turn to give other people ulcers."

What does all of this mean to you as a manager seeking to motivate your subordinates to do better work? Simply this— when you can, show your employees job opportunities, job environment, and a supervisory attitude which helps them satisfy their higher and current needs. When you do this, you are offering them benefits which they can respond to. These are real needs which cannot be met by a process of manipulation or window dressing.

One final comment is important. Most of these higher needs relate to the job itself. Yet rewards typically provided an employee, such as wages and fringe benefits, can only be used to satisfy the employee's needs when he leaves the job. Wages, for example, cannot be spent at work. For many wage earners, therefore, work is perceived as a form of punishment which is the price to be paid for various kinds of satisfaction away from the job.

It is for these reasons that Herzberg and others after questioning thousands of employees at all levels, conclude that for most people, most of the time, money is not a positive job motivator.[3] More money does not affect the job itself. Absence of money leads to dissatisfaction, but salary increases do not necessarily rate high on the list of factors that lead to extreme job satisfaction.

Under today's conditions, management has provided relatively well for the satisfaction of the basic and safety needs. Since these needs are satisfied, they no longer become motivators of behavior. Theory Y says that management's job is therefore to provide opportunities at work to satisfy the ego needs. Otherwise people will be deprived and problems will arise. Furthermore, by making possible the satisfaction of lower-level needs, management has deprived itself of the ability to use the control devices on which the conventional assumptions of Theory X has taught it to rely: rewards, promises, incentives, or threats and other coercive devices.

The Theory Y approach is a necessity today in many organizations, if the organization is to run smoothly.

[3] For a summary of this view, see Frederick Herzberg, "One more time: How do you motivate employees?" *Harvard Business Review*, January–February 1968.

Part **2**

Structure

The second blue chip heading of the Behind the Words system, and thus the second side of the Behind the Words triangle, is Structure. Under this heading are collected the key steps and guides concerning the planning and organizing necessary for successful management communications. The Structure heading has two red chip steps:

    Step 3   Build a Poker Chip Outline
    Step 4   Plan a Visible Structure

Step 3
Build a Poker Chip Outline

Every message has a structure. The successful business communication should have a tight, clear, sound structure. This Step 3 explains how to build such a structure for a message.

The three guides under this Step 3 are as follows:

- Identify your poker chips
- Arrange in appropriate sequence
- Decide your opening and closing

The following summary shows how these guides are used:

To identify your poker chips, identify first your main ideas, or blue chips; then identify the subordinate, or red chip, ideas that belong under each blue chip, and, if appropriate, the white chip ideas that belong under each red chip.

For convenience, consider the opening of your message as your first blue chip and the closing as your last blue chip, even though each may be shorter in length than the blue chips constituting the body of your message and even though the opening and closing may stand apart from the body of the message. If you have an opening or closing at a subordinate level, again consider each as a part of the poker chips constituting that level.

To arrange your poker chips in appropriate sequence after you have identified them, first arrange the blue chips in the sequence you want to present them; then continue by arranging the red chips and white chips in the appropriate sequences for each. Possible sequences include point first, point last, straight line, and rambling.

To decide your opening and closing, review the People steps and the poker chip outline you have built up to this point. Select an opening that establishes contact; previews the subject; and summarizes key facts, findings and recommendations. The closing you choose, if any, depends greatly on the type of message.

IDENTIFY YOUR POKER CHIPS

The poker chip analogy serves four useful purposes:

- It provides us with a set of handy terms to use in the outlining process ("blue chips" and "red chips" are shorter terms to work with and easier concepts to visualize than "major ideas" and "subordinate ideas").
- It distinguishes the outlining technique described here from the elaborate, formal, and dreary outlining process so often taught in school and college.
- It helps us focus on the vital need for an outline that sorts ideas into their varying levels of importance and collects subordinate ideas under their appropriate main headings.
- It helps us remember the necessity for unity because a poker chip stands for one and only one unit.

To start building a poker chip outline for a message, identify first your main ideas. These are your blue chips; write each down in a few words. Next, identify the red chip ideas that belong under each blue chip; then, if appropriate, identify the white chip ideas that belong under each red chip. Write down the red and white chips, again in a few words.

Your poker chip outline at this point should be informal, tentative, and brief. Keep it this way. This is your working outline from which you will write or speak your message. Don't let the outline become bogged down in detail. The process of writing or speaking generates new and frequently better ideas; an outline that is too detailed must often be discarded, lest it become a stultifying burden that inhibits creativity.

Avoid the elaborate, detailed, formal outline so often taught in school or college, with its Roman numerals for the main ideas, capital letters for the first level of subordination, etc. Such outlines are usually prepared by the student after the paper is written to satisfy the requirement of a teacher. Perhaps they are valuable as a means of training orderly thinking, but they are seldom useful in helping organize a message. In fact, many of us avoid the outlining process because of unpleasant memories of the tedious work involved in preparing these elaborate, formal outlines.

The process of identifying your poker chips and of building a poker chip outline is described here for the more complex written message because this necessarily requires pencil and paper and a more complex outline; but don't neglect the poker chip outline for the shorter written message or for any face-to-face communications. This less-elaborate process will take you less time, but is equally important.

For example, if you are answering a letter, you may be able to identify the blue chips for your answer by simply underlining the key points in the incoming letter. This then becomes the outline for your answer. Likewise, if you are about to meet with one or more subordinates, superiors, associates, or customers, take at least a few moments first to identify your poker chips and build in your mind a poker chip outline of the points you want to cover during the meeting. Unless you are sure you will remember these, write them down. This then becomes your personal agenda.

As you identify your poker chips, whether for a complex written message or a brief meeting with another person, other thoughts and ideas will come to mind. Write these down before you forget them. When you do this, you are effectively using the creative and intuitive side of your mind. Some of our best ideas come to us suddenly, without warning, and leave us just as suddenly and with equally little warning. Unless we record these frequently valuable ideas, they are easily forgotten. Innovative managers have learned to listen to the creative side of their mind and to write down sudden hunches immediately, without attempting to evaluate them.

After you have prepared your first informal and tentative poker chip outline, stop, look at it, and think about it. Have you omitted anything you should include? Have you included anything you should omit?

To help answer these questions, review the People steps. Start with the People questions—What is your purpose?, Who is involved?, What do they want? Are you sure of your purpose, and does your outline accurately reflect this purpose? Does your outline consider all the people in your audience and what you know about these people? Does it consider what they will want from this message?

What motivators can you use to help you achieve the results you seek? What can you do to catch and hold attention? What can you do to show your audience the why? What are the benefits to them of acting your way? What are the sales motivators? What are the job motivators? Are you appealing to the higher-level needs of your audience?

Some of these questions you can answer only tentatively at this point since your outline is not yet finished, but it is well to raise them now.

Finally, check your list of poker chips for unity. Be sure

that you have one idea and only one idea per poker chip. Don't let one heading cover two or more separate ideas that should be broken out under separate headings. A poker chip represents a unit of meaning; it is not like a piece of putty which can be easily made larger or smaller.

ARRANGE IN APPROPRIATE SEQUENCE

Having identified your poker chips, next decide the sequence in which you want to arrange them; i.e., if you have three blue chips, which is first, which is second, which is third? In doing this, consider your purpose, the substance of the message, and the particular audiences you seek. Your arranging should start with the blue chips and then move to the red chips and the white chips (and further, of course, if your outline has more than three levels).

There are four basic sequences in which ideas can be presented in any message or any portion of any message:

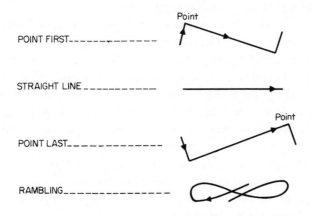

In the point-first sequence, the point is stated soon after the opening and is then followed by the supporting facts, sometimes with a summary at the end.

The straight-line sequence follows a logical order, but not

necessarily one which puts the most important ideas first or last.

Point last is the opposite of point first.

The rambling sequence wanders from one idea to the next in no apparent order.

A message or portion of a message may combine two or more of these sequences.

Point First

This sequence presents first at each poker chip level the point or most important ideas of the message. Sometimes a message has a single point; sometimes several ideas stand out as the most important.

Remember to decide importance in the terms of your purpose and in terms of what your audience wants. For example, the methods you used to collect or analyze your facts may seem of real importance to you and to be deserving of real recognition in your message; but to most of your audience, these will be of minor interest at best.

The point-first arrangement recognizes that a business audience, for an oral or written message, is composed of busy people. They are seldom listening or reading simply to be entertained or to admire your polished prose; rather, they are reading or listening for meaning; they want to decide what action, if any, they should take as a result of your message.

The word "business" originally meant "the state of being busy"—thus, a businessman is busy. Don't irritate your audience or risk losing their attention by not getting to the point as soon as possible; tell them the point early in the message so that they can then judge your message in terms of the previously stated point.

But, you object, if I tell my reader the point early in the message and if he disagrees with it, either he will stop reading or he will be so prejudiced that he will not read my facts with an open mind; therefore I should avoid a point-first sequence of ideas. This familiar argument overlooks the important fact that few of us have the time or inclination to read a business message all the way through from beginning to end without knowing the point of the message or the direction the writer is taking us. Most of us, after having read a few sentences of a message with an obscure point, will skip or scan until we find the point and then come back to read the message in the light of what we now know to be the point.

The writer who attempts to obscure or hide his point, or to present his facts first and lead up to a point gradually, risks irritating and wasting the time of the busy reader who wants to know the point first, before reading the body of the message. If you question this statement, check your own reading habits as you empty your in-box. If you cannot quickly see the point of a message, do you methodically read it through, analyzing and considering the pros and cons of the facts or arguments presented, without knowing what the writer's conclusions will be? Or do you skim and scan until you find the conclusion and then come back and, if necessary, read the body of the message?

This leads to another important reason for the point-first sequence. Many readers or listeners are interested only in the point of a message, with perhaps a few key supporting facts. They do not have the time or the need for the details. Often these readers are the people near or at the top of the ladder, whose in-boxes are so overflowing with reports, letters, and proposals and whose calendars are so filled with meetings that they must take a briefcase home every night. These men welcome the point-first sequence because it saves them time; as a result, they are likely to remember favorably writers or speakers who follow this sequence.

Point first is equally important in the oral message. If you are reporting to me on the progress of a particular matter, I don't want to be held in suspense while you recite to me all the various facts, anecdotes, and episodes leading up to your point. You aren't telling me a joke or a detective story. You are reporting on a business situation. Come to the point quickly and then develop the facts.

Some listeners will be patient with the speaker who attempts to present the facts first without stating the point, but others will cut the speaker short with such impatient questions as "What's your point?" or "What are you getting at?" If this happens to you, let it be a warning that you are not using a point-first sequence.

Point first does not require that you state your point bluntly in the first words of your first sentence. There is always time for courtesy and for brief background explanations.

Point first is the preferred sequence of ideas for most business messages, particularly at the blue chip level, but it is certainly not the only sequence. Let's look now at the others.

Point Last

In this sequence the writer or speaker presents his facts first, working up gradually to his conclusion. He hopes that his audience will stay with him, eagerly absorbing his presentation, until he makes his point.

The point-last sequence is both appropriate and necessary in telling a mystery story or a joke, as there is no suspense or nothing to laugh at if we know the point or the plot from the beginning.

A salesman explaining the merits of his product to a new prospect usually uses a combination of point first and point last. The point, or purpose, of the salesman's call should be known to the prospect as soon as the salesman introduces himself. (The salesman who tries to hide his true purpose risks dealing with an angry prospect.) Also, many successful salesmen summarize their key sales points before starting their detailed presentation and thus use a point-first approach here also.

But the oral presentation itself is necessarily point last,

since to a salesman the point is to close the sale, and, once the sale is closed, the presentation is ended.

Occasionally a point-last approach is necessary in either writing or speaking, if you know your audience will jump to conclusions as soon as they hear your point and therefore will not allow you to develop the facts. Before choosing point last for this reason, consider whether your audience will wait for you to finish if you use a point-last approach, or whether they will become impatient and demand to know your point either by interrupting (if you are speaking) or by scanning until they find your point (if you are writing).

Point last remains the traditional approach for the scientific, engineering, or academic paper, particularly the paper written by the faculty member seeking his next promotion. The scientific method requires a disciplined process of purely inductive reasoning; a paper describing research which follows the scientific method should therefore present the facts one by one, each fact inexorably leading to the next, until the conclusion of the research is described.

Editors of learned journals are increasingly recognizing that the point-last sequence does not lead to an interesting paper and does not satisfy the busy reader's need for a quick summary of the article. Many editors now require not only an abstract at the beginning, but also a summary at the start of the text of the article. The summary helps each reader decide whether this particular paper is of interest to him, and, if so, to what extent. (The difficulty with using the abstract alone is that it is often printed in small type and written as one long sentence, with too much compression of ideas and at too high a level of abstraction to be easily understood.)

Academic papers often follow the point-last sequence for another highly practical reason. The assistant professor, writing his paper under the "publish or perish" doctrine, must write it to be promoted. His audience is therefore the head of his department; he may not really care whether anyone else reads it. The head of his department is usually more interested in his junior's research than in his conclusion. Therefore a sequence that presents the facts first, and the point last, may well be a "point-first" arrangement for the head of the department.

Straight Line

This sequence of ideas follows a logical pattern but does not attempt to emphasize any particular idea by placing it first or last in the sequence. Typical examples would include a chronological sequence for reporting on a meeting or business trip; a geographical or functional sequence for discussing common problems involving several departments or plant locations; an alphabetical sequence for discussing qualifications of candidates for a particular job; and a step-by-step sequence for presenting an instruction, regulation, directive, or procedure.

Because a straight-line sequence avoids emphasizing the most important ideas in the sequence, it is usually best combined with a point-first opening. Thus, if I have visited all the regional offices in my organization to inspect their hiring practices, and now must report to you on my findings and recommendations, I should probably start with a point-first summary of key findings and recommendations, and continue with a detailed report, following a geographical sequence. Likewise, if I am instructing you, orally or in writing, on how to perform a particular task, I should first set the stage by explaining why this task is necessary, or where it fits into a larger picture, before proceeding with the detailed step-by-step instruction.

Rambling

Nothing can be said in favor of a rambling sequence of ideas; unfortunately it is a sequence that we see too often, perhaps as a result of laziness, haste, or lack of training on the communicator's part or perhaps from a basic lack of confidence in his ability to express ideas clearly. No matter how pressed we are for time, we can and always should find at least a few moments to plan our message first.

DECIDE YOUR OPENING AND CLOSING

The last step in the process of building a poker chip outline is to decide the type of opening and closing you want. You may well ask—why wait until the end of the outlining process to decide on your opening? The answer is that this usually works out better because you can't really decide on your opening until you see the shape of your ideas; and you can't see this shape until you are well into your poker chip outline.

An effective opening is essential for a successful message. It should establish contact, preview the subject, highlight its importance to the receiver, and usually it should summarize key facts, findings, and recommendations. Above all, it should catch and hold attention. If your opening is so dull that you lose your reader or listener at the very start, you risk never getting his full attention again, and thus you greatly decrease your chances of accomplishing your purpose in communicating.

The need for a closing, and the type of closing to choose, varies greatly according to the type of message. A closing may summarize the content of the message, and thus repeat the opening (often desirable in oral messages or in long reports); it may be a call to action; or it may not be related to the substance of the message but rather may identify who has the next move (for example, "Please report to me on this next Thursday," "I will call you next week to discuss this further."); or it may be omitted entirely.

Discussed below are suggested openings for three types of written messages.

The Short Letter or Internal Memo

To open a short letter or internal memo, establish contact by referring to the previous communication; then state or preview the subject. In internal memos, and sometimes in letters, these two items may be covered in the heading; for example—

> TO: Peter C. Cohen
> FROM: Walter M. Brown
> Reference: Your memo of July 12
> Subject: The weak widget problem

In a letter outside the organization, these two items can often be covered in a one-sentence opening paragraph; for example:

> Dear Mr. Cohen:
> Thank you for your letter of July 12 concerning the weak widget problem.

The objection is sometimes raised that this opening sentence is unnecessary and therefore should be omitted if Cohen is, for example, a customer or member of the public who has written you only one letter. Strictly speaking, it is unnecessary in this case to remind Cohen of the date of his letter; but this date reference is always helpful for your own files and will become necessary if Cohen continues to write and you continue to answer. After a while, it will not be clear which letter answers which. Likewise, a brief statement of the subject tells every reader at the outset what the letter is about, and thus saves reader time. Finally, this standard opening starts with the phrase "Thank you for your letter. . . ." This courteous opening is widely used today and is desirable in every case except where the courtesy would be obviously inappropriate.

In addition to establishing contact and stating the subject, the opening of a short letter or internal memo should also, whenever possible, summarize the key facts, findings, and recommendations and show their importance to the audience, or, at the least, tell the reader what he may expect to find in the communication. In the example above, the summary might appear in another short paragraph:

Dear Mr. Cohen:

Thank you for your letter of July 12 concerning the weak widget problem.

For the three reasons stated in this letter, our engineers recommend that you replace all your widgets with our new Model X-24. We are shipping you a full supply of the new model by air express today.

Reports and Proposals: the One-Page Summary

If you are writing a report or proposal that will be longer than about four pages, plan to write a one-page summary. Include the body of the report or proposal as an attachment, preferably with its own cover page. (If it is shorter than four pages, follow the opening suggested above for an internal memo.) Be sure to include the following in the summary:

- Establish contact and state the subject (as in the short letter or internal memo).
- State your purpose, preferably worded as a statement of a problem, an objective, or a question.
- Set the stage. Summarize key facts, whether recognized at the outset or developed during your study of the problem. State any important assumptions and any criteria—standards, tests, rules—used in analyzing the problem. Show the alternate solutions or approaches you considered.
- State your key findings and recommendations. Distinguish between these, if appropriate. Show their importance to your audience. If this is a proposal, state the benefits to be expected.

- Refer to your detailed discussion, either by summarizing it or (if that is impractical) by listing section headings for the detailed discussion.
- Close the one-page summary by making it clear who has the next move (i.e., what action is expected of whom?).

In terms of the poker chip outline, the one-page summary follows a point-first sequence and is the first blue chip. The one-page summary is helpful to every reader, but it is particularly designed for the people at the top of the ladder who have neither the time nor the desire to read in detail every proposal or report which demands their attention. Many men at the top demand one-page summaries and refuse to read any report or proposal without one.

When Gen. George C. Marshall took over as Chief of Staff of the United States Army (and, in effect, became the senior military officer for the Allied forces in World War II), he found that he was overwhelmed by urgent reports demanding his attention. He therefore required that all reports addressed to him be summarized on one page, and, to handle the interim problem, he hired several lawyers whose job it was to prepare a one-page summary of every report addressed to him. Probably as a result of Marshall's insistence during World War II, the one-page summary is today required in many government agencies and large corporations for reports headed for the top. (Unfortunately, the requirement of a one-page summary seems to fade out for reports that are aimed only at an upper-middle or middle level.)

Here is how you can usefully apply the one-page summary:

If you are a senior official and you must read pages of reports and proposals, demand one-page summaries. Not only does it save you hours, but it forces your subordinates, as they write their reports, to discipline their thinking.

If you are expecting a lengthy proposal from a supplier,

consultant, or other organization, require them to furnish a one-page summary, including the expected benefits. If your organization prepares lengthy proposals for prospective clients or customers, demand that proposal writers include a one-page summary, again including the expected benefits. You cannot hurt your chances of making the sale; rather, you can expect to improve them.

On the other hand, if you are a writer rather than a reader of reports and proposals, make it a firm practice to always prepare a one-page summary. You not only improve your chances of getting the action you seek from your message, you also are likely to be remembered with favor by those who read your message.

Instructions: Show Them the Why

The best opening in instruction writing (procedures, directives, rules, regulations, etc.) is a specialized application of Show them the why—the second guide under Step 2.

To do this, show the user where the instruction fits into the larger picture of the job as a whole, or tell him why the procedure is necessary. Also, give him an overview of the instruction as a whole, so that he will not be forced to move blindly from step to step, without any clear idea of the end result.

The next four cases illustrate the application of the guides for the poker chip outline.

CASE 5   THE LEAKY PLUMBING RISERS

The memo that follows was written by the plant engineer of a machine tool company to the plant manager, who found it on his desk when he returned from a business trip. The plant manager blew up when he read it because it represented to him one more example of the muddled thinking and lazy habits which had characterized his plant engineer. (The manager realized also that part of the problem lay in his own failure on previous occasions to demand better performance.) Here is the memo:

TO: Mr. Smith, Plant Manager
FROM: Mr. Jones, Plant Engineer
SUBJECT: Plumbing Risers

Recently we had trouble with the phone lines in the lower section of the main building. The telephone company came and investigated and found that the riser going through the Old Wing was badly corroded and leaking down into the telephone panel near Mr. Winter's office. As a result of his investigations, Mr. Dougherty asked the plumbing contractor to give us a quotation on replacing the bad risers. The first quote, attached, indicates the cost will be some $3,513.

The second quote refers to a riser in the ceiling of one of the labs in the Research Center. This riser was found to be in poor shape when it was constructed but we did not replace it at that time with the hope that money would be forthcoming for a major plumbing renovation. While we are still waiting for funds for such a renovation, the pipes are becoming more brittle and corroded. The result is that the wall and ceiling of the lab are badly stained and we continually keep a bucket under the riser in order to catch the steady drip coming from it. As you can see the price of $6,324 combined with the $3,513 of the other quote means that we have gotten into a position where the plumbing has deteriorated completely and we must prepare ourselves for the expenditure of substantial sums.

The source of the monies to make these two no longer urgent but extremely urgent, bordering on emergency repairs, has not been set aside in any budget. However, I feel we can ill afford to delay more than a few weeks before acting. It may be that a special dispensation from the president should be sought to make these repairs since there is no budget which can afford to take a $10,000 add-on. I would like to discuss that particular problem with you at our next meeting.

Let's analyze this horrible example of an internal memo by applying the Behind the Words system as developed to this point. It becomes immediately obvious as we do this that the memo is almost totally lacking in structure. The writer has rambled back and forth through his subject without any attempt to pull his ideas together and present them in an orderly fashion. His haphazard punctuation compounds the problem.

Apply the three People Questions to the memo and further problems and weaknesses are highlighted. What is Jones's purpose here? Does he really want to discuss the problem at the next meeting? What is there left to discuss? The facts, although scattered and rambling, are in the memo. Jones's purpose should have been to obtain Smith's immediate approval to hire the plumber.

Jones also totally failed to consider his audience and what that audience wants. Smith was fed up; he had already received from Jones too many muddled memos like this. Perhaps Smith was too much of a Theory Y–type manager, but this memo was in fact the final straw that caused Smith to seriously consider whether Jones should remain as plant engineer.

The first step in analyzing the content of the memo is to pull out of these three muddled paragraphs the key facts. On the next page, these have been underlined and numbered.

TO: Mr. Smith, Plant Manager
FROM: Mr. Jones, Plant Engineer
SUBJECT: Plumbing Risers

1.
Recently we had trouble with the phone lines in the lower section of the main building. The telephone company came and investigated and found that the *riser going through the Old Wing was badly corroded* and

leaking down into the telephone panel near Mr. Winter's office. As a result of his investigations, Mr. Dougherty asked the plumbing contractor to give us a quotation on replacing the bad riser. The first quote, attached, indi-

2. cates the *cost will be some $3,513.*

3. { The second quote refers to a *riser in the ceiling of one of the labs in the Research Center.* This riser was found to be in poor shape when it was constructed but we did not replace it at that time with the hope that money would be forthcoming for a major plumbing renovation. While we are still waiting for funds for such a renovation, the pipes are becoming *more brittle and corroded.* The result is that the wall and ceiling of the lab are badly stained and we continually *keep a bucket under the riser* in order to catch the steady drip coming from it. As you

4. can see the price of *$6,324* combined with the $3,513 of the other quote means that we have gotten into a position

5. where the *plumbing has deteriorated completely* and we must prepare ourselves for the expenditure of substantial sums.

6. The source of the monies to make these two no longer urgent but extremely urgent, bordering on *emergency repairs,* has not been set aside in any budget. However, I feel we can ill afford to delay more than a few weeks

7. before acting. It may be that a *special dispensation from the president* should be sought to make these repairs since there is no budget which can afford to take a $10,000

8. add-on. *I would like to discuss that particular problem with you at our next meeting.*

Put these key ideas together in coherent, streamlined form, and the result is along these lines:

- The plumbing riser into the Old Wing is badly corroded and leaking. The estimated cost to replace it is $3,513.
- The riser in the ceiling of one of the Research Center labs is becoming increasingly brittle and corroded. We must keep a bucket under it to catch the steady drip. The estimated cost to repair it is $6,324.

- Our plumbing has deteriorated completely, and we must prepare ourselves for substantial expenditures.
- The two repairs are emergencies, but there is no money in the budget. We may need a special dispensation from the president. I would like to discuss this with you at our next meeting.

Revising the memo into this abbreviated form helps us to see more of the sloppy thinking in the original. For example, Jones starts by talking about the phones as though the problem were there, but then we find that the problem concerns the plumbing riser. The fact that the telephone company found the leak is not material, unless Jones means to say the leak could also lead to telephone service problems. If so, Jones should have said this directly.

The start of the second paragraph is a little clearer, although rambling. Obviously, the riser in the lab of the ceiling needs to be replaced. The first "it" in the second sentence is confusing. Jones was referring here to the Research Center and not the riser.

The last three lines of the second paragraph are confusing indeed; this was one of the points in the memo that particularly angered Smith. Does this mean that substantial additional plumbing repairs will be necessary? Or is Jones simply reiterating what he has already said? If so, how substantial and how urgent are they, and what does Jones propose to do about it?

In the third paragraph, if Jones means that this is an emergency, why doesn't he say so in the fewest possible words? If it is an emergency, is it safe to wait several weeks before acting? What more is there for Jones to discuss in his next meeting with Smith? If this is an emergency, the money must be found and the pipes must be repaired.

The last sentence of the memo is an excellent example of incomplete staff work (often called "delegation upward"). Jones should have assumed the responsibility of asking Smith to approve the $10,000 at once, so that Jones could go ahead and contract for repairs. Instead, Jones simply presented the facts and then dumped the problem in Smith's lap. This is delegation upward because, in effect, Jones is saying to Smith, "Here's the problem, boss; now you tell me what to do."

Let's revise the memo, reducing it to the barest essentials necessary to full inform Smith of the problem and to state Jones's findings and recommendations. The memo then might read as follows:

Subject: $10,000 Needed for Emergency Plumbing Repairs

(opening)
blue
chip 1

We have recently discovered two plumbing risers that are leaking badly and require emergency repairs. The cost of these repairs is approximately $10,000. There is no money in the budget.

blue
chip 2

The first riser, going through the Old Wing, is badly corroded and leaking into the telephone panel near Mr. Winter's office. The telephone company found this in investigating problems with telephone service. Mr. Dougherty has obtained an estimate from the plumbing contractor (attached) of $3,513.

blue
chip 3

The second riser is in the ceiling of one of the labs in the Research Center. When the Center was built, we found this riser to be in poor shape but put off replacing it until a major plumbing renovation. In the meantime, the pipe is becoming increasingly brittle and corroded, so that we must keep a bucket under it to catch the steady drip. The estimate for repairing this (also attached) is $6,324.

blue
chip 4

I believe these are emergency repairs and should be completed promptly. As stated, there is no money in the budget. Please authorize me to go ahead with these repairs so that I may contract with the plumbers as soon as possible.

blue
chip 5

The need for these two emergency repairs raises the obvious question of whether other plumbing risers are in equally poor shape, and therefore whether we will soon need a major plumbing renovation. I am investigating this question now and will report to you on it within the next month.

The marginal comments show the poker chip outline for this memo. Note that Jones is no longer delegating upward; he presents the problem of leaky pipes, states the obvious and necessary solution of repairing them, and asks for approval because there is no money in the budget. The last paragraph relates to another subject but is included here so that Smith will know Jones has not overlooked this larger problem.

CASE 6   THE REPAIR SHOP REQUISITION FORM

C. B. Stennis was the energetic new operations manager at the Monterey plant of a manufacturing company. Soon after he started his new job, he found that the repair shop was repairing production machines without requiring a written requisition. Most of the foremen, knowing this, did not bother to fill out requisition forms, except perhaps on a major repair. Downtime records for several important production machines were therefore unreliable; thus Stennis could not find out which machines had the best service record.

Stennis therefore sent to all foremen the memo which appears below, attaching a copy of the existing repair-shop requisition form. He was disappointed to find that nothing much happened as a result of his memo; a check several weeks later revealed that the foremen still were not using the form and the repair shop still was not insisting on it. Here is his memo:

MONTEREY PLANT to: ALL FOREMEN
SUBJECT: *PREVENTIVE MAINTENANCE*
          REPAIR SHOP REQUISITION

1. All work requested of the maintenance department must be requisitioned on the "Repair Shop Requisition" form which is initiated and signed by the department foreman or person delegated by him.

2. The portions of the form that are to be filled out by the foreman include:

> Department
> Date
> Priority
> Mach. No.
> Description of work
> And his signature

3. The "Completed by" and "Hours" columns, as well as the "Reason for failure" section are for the maintenance department's use and are left blank by the foreman.

4. Disregard the "Breakdown" and "Routine" blocks on the form and insert the proper priority just above the word "Breakdown," according to the attached schedule.

5. Make out the form in duplicate. Send, or take, the original to the maintenance department and retain the carbon copy for your record.

6. The form is primarily used for scheduling maintenance personnel, but will also be used as time sheets and machine history records including repair frequency and cost.

7. If work other than on a production machine is required, use the word "Building" or "Equipment." "Building" means any part of the building structure, walls, floors, ceilings, posts, etc. "Equipment" means everything other than the building structure, such as lights, electrical wiring, hand trucks, benches, cabinets, elevators, water fountains, and all other equipment other than production machines.

8. Any questions in regard to the use of these forms or the priority system can be directed to the writer.

C. B. Stennis

```
┌─────────────────────────────────────────────────────────────────┐
│                  REPAIR SHOP REQUISITION                          │
│                  ─────────────────────────                        │
│                                                                   │
│  DEPT. _____           ☐ BREAKDOWN                     │
│                                                                   │
│  DATE _____            ☐ ROUTINE                       │
├──────────┬─────────────────────────────────┬──────────┬──────────┤
│  MACH.   │                                 │  COMP.   │          │
│   NO.    │   DESCRIPTION OF WORK           │   BY     │  HOURS   │
├──────────┼─────────────────────────────────┼──────────┼──────────┤
│          │                                 │          │          │
│          │                                 │          │          │
│          │                                 │          │          │
│          │                                 │          │          │
├──────────┴─────────────────────────────────┴──────────┴──────────┤
│     REASON FOR FAILURE                                            │
│     ──────────────────              FOREMAN _____        │
│  ☐ NORMAL WEAR         ☐ OTHER-EXPLAIN      ───────────────       │
│  ☐ LACK OF LUBRICATION              ──────────────────────────    │
│  ☐ CARELESSNESS                     ──────────────────────────    │
│  ☐ NEW CONSTRUCTION                 ──────────────────────────    │
│                                     ──────────────────────────    │
│                                     ──────────────                │
└─────────────────────────────────────────────────────────────────┘
```

The Behind the Words system, as developed to this point, will be used to analyze Stennis's problem and discover why his memo failed.

To start, apply the People Questions. What was Stennis's purpose? This is clearly stated—Stennis wanted the form to be used for each repair job.

Who is involved? The answer to this question offers the first clue as to why the memo failed. It is written to foremen who, rather than spending their day sitting at a desk, are on the floor, on their feet, dealing with the men and machines they supervise. Foremen often resist paper work; filling out forms and reports is looked on as an unpleasant chore that interferes with their real job. Also, many foremen lack adequate or quiet desk or filing space. Yet, the instructions for the use of the form are separate from the form itself and thus are not likely to be handy when the foremen is filling out the form.

What do they want? The answer to the second question leads us to the answer to the third question. If a form is necessary, then the foreman wants a form that is easy to fill out on the floor of the shop, without referring to confusing or poorly worded instructions which are not a part of the form.

As is so often true, both the form and the instructions are writer-oriented, not user-oriented. Stennis failed to step into the foremen's shoes and to look at the problem from their point of view instead of his.

Continuing with the Behind the Words analysis, does Stennis use motivators in this memo? Does this memo catch and hold the foremen's attention? Does it show them why the form is necessary and thus motivate them to fill out the form each time? The negative answers to these questions suggest two more reasons why the memo failed.

Now let's look at the structure of the memo. There are eight numbered paragraphs, and therefore the apparent structure is eight blue chips—eight separate independent ideas of equal importance. In fact, this is not the true structure of ideas in the memo and thus represents another area of confusion.

After sorting the blue and red chips, the memo could be rewritten as follows:

blue
chip 1
(opening;
the why)

1. The repair shop requisition form is not being used. This form is necessary to help us schedule repair jobs efficiently. Also it provides a history of downtime on production machines, so that we can identify machines that are in need of major overhaul or are not working efficiently.

blue
chip 2
(instructions)

2. Each foreman (or person authorized by the foreman) who requisitions work from the repair shop will complete the form for each requisition, as follows:

2A. Make out the form in duplicate. Send, or take, the original to the maintenance department, and keep the carbon for your records.

2B. Fill in the following items on the form:
Dept.
Date
Priority
Machine No.
Description of Work
Foreman's Signature

2C. Leave blank these headings: Comp. by, Hours, and Reason for failure.

2D. Disregard the Breakdown and Routine blocks, and insert the proper priority just above the word "breakdown," according to the attached schedule.

2E. If work is required other than on a production machine, insert "building" or "equipment" under the heading Mach. No. "Building" means any part of the building structure, walls, floors, ceilings, posts, etc. "Equipment" means everything other than building structure or production machines, including lights, electrical wiring, hand trucks, benches, cabinets, elevators, water fountains, etc.

Please contact me if you have any questions regarding this form or the priority system.

This is a better memo, but the form itself needs revision. Whenever possible, instructions for using a form should appear on the form itself. Also, the form is not up to date (the Breakdown and Routine boxes no longer apply).

Stennis had in fact decided not to revise the form because he had 2,000 copies in the supply room—enough for two years at the current rate of use. But paper is cheaper than the reader's time. Stennis saved a few dollars by not reprinting the form; and lost many more dollars because the failure to use the form led to inefficient scheduling of repairs and poor downtime records. Perhaps these lost dollars were more difficult to measure, but surely they would have been more significant.

CASE 7   ELECTRIC POWER FOR STRONG MANUFACTURING COMPANY

The following is a letter written by a power company salesman to one of his customers:

Mr. John Peters
Vice-president of Manufacturing
Strong Manufacturing Company

Dear John:

During our recent conversation regarding your power situation and the alternatives that are available to you, I want to confirm the recommendations that were made by Mr. Bennett and me so that you may examine them and pick out what you think is best for your particular situation.

1.) As you know, for some time your plant has been available for our large power Rate No. 107 with savings approximating $5,000 annually over your present purchase of power. With the new loads that you plan within the next two years, I estimate that this savings will become approximately $7,000–$8,000 annually. In order to be eligible for large power Rate No. 107, our company must be relieved of any investment on the customer's property. This means that we will negotiate to sell equipment on your property now owned by the Central State Power Company. I estimate that the sale price will be approximately $5,000; however, I will confirm this at a later date. If you should elect to purchase the facilities and accept Rate No. 107, which we would strongly recommend, then it would be to your advantage to purchase and own additional transformers placed as closely to the load as possible to minimize long, secondary runs and voltage drop. With the power requirements that you anticipate, this would mean approximately 750 kVA in transformers, and I estimate this to cost about $7,000, not installed. This is the plan that we would heartily recommend.

2.) If, for reasons of your own, you did not wish to purchase the facilities and elected to remain on present Rate No. 100, we would then increase the size of the present transformer bank, which is now operating at full capacity, at the present location, to a size consistently with the present and proposed loads. This then would mean long, *costly* secondary runs from the vault to your furnaces.

Please let me know at your earliest convenience how you would like this problem handled. The delivery on transformers is quite lengthy, and the more lead time you can give us the better.

Very truly yours,

Walter R. Walters
Industrial Sales Engineer

This letter does not present as many problems as the memos in Cases 5 and 6. Nonetheless, it is one more example of a rambling, wordy message that needs to be tidied up. The letter was perhaps adequate to do the job it was designed to do, but surely it could have been more effective.

Walters knew that he, as a salesman for a power company, was essentially in a monopoly position; perhaps he didn't feel it necessary to try too hard. (This attitude can appear whenever there is no real competition for the product or service a salesman is selling.) Thus, the letter is not only rambling and wordy, but, in the third paragraph, is somewhat condescending. The phrase "If, for reasons of your own, you did not wish to purchase the facilities . . ." seems to say in effect, "If you are so stupid that you do not accept our recommendations. . . ." The failure of the first and second clauses in the first sentence to tie together results from careless writing.

Another muddy sentence is found in the second paragraph:

"This means that we will negotiate to sell equipment on your property now owned by the Central State Power Company." Walters confuses the reader because the Central State Power Company is his own company. First he talks about his own company by using the pronoun "we," and then he refers to it by name as though it were a third party.

What is the message of this letter? What are the blue chips? What result does the writer seek? Let's analyze it, starting with the People Questions.

Walters' purpose is clear—he wants to have the company change over to the large power rate.

Who is involved? An industrial customer, or more specifically, the vice-president who will make the decision.

What do they want? Probably Peters would have liked to have received in this letter a summary, well-organized and easy to read, of the advantages and disadvantages of changing over to the new basis. He did not receive this because the letter is poorly structured.

What are the motivators? The letter is short enough so that it presents no serious problems in catching and holding attention. Peters can be assumed to be sufficiently concerned with this question so that he will read the letter. The sales motivators are financial. The new power rate will save money, although the amount of the savings is hard to calculate from this letter. Walters first talks of saving $5,000 annually at the present rate of purchase of power. With new loads within the next two years, the saving becomes $7,000 to $8,000, but Strong must sell its present transformers and purchase new transformers at an apparent net cost of $2,000. Whether or not this figure is included in the $7,000 estimated annual savings is scarcely clear.

Here is a revised letter, with the poker chip outline shown in the margin; certain assumptions were made for facts missing in the original letter:

Dear John:

At our meeting in your office on March 13, you

blue
chip 1
(opening)

asked me to confirm the recommendations Mr. Bennett and I made to you regarding your power situation and the alternatives available.

blue
chip 2

We recommend that you change over to large power Rate No. 107.

(summary;
benefits)

(cost)

We estimate that the savings to you at your present rate of power use would approximate $5,000 annually. Considering the new loads you plan in the next two years, this savings would increase to approximately $7,000 to $8,000 annually. The changeover would require a net capital investment of about $2,000. ($7,000 for new transformers less $5,000 sales price of present transformers.)

blue
chip 3

Rate No. 107 requires that our company be relieved of any investment on the customer's property. At present, we own the transformers and other equipment in your vault. We will be pleased to seek a purchaser for this equipment; we estimate a sale price of approximately $5,000. We will confirm this estimate later.

blue
chip 4

In place of these transformers, you should purchase new transformers, to be placed as closely to the load as possible to minimize long secondary runs and voltage drop. For the power requirements you anticipate, you would need approximately 750 kVA in transformers at an estimated cost of $7,000, not installed. If you decide not to change over to Rate 107, but rather to remain on your present Rate 100, we would then increase the size of the present transformer bank, which is now operating at full capacity. We would do this at the present site. This would mean long, costly secondary runs from the bank to your furnaces.

Please let me know your decision at your earliest

blue   convenience. There is at present a six month's
chip 5   lead time for transformer deliveries, so the more
(closing)   time you can give us the better.

The revised letter follows a structure that is appropriate for many letters to customers, whether sales or for other purposes. The first paragraph establishes contact and states the subject. The second paragraph summarizes the proposal and states the benefits. The third and fourth paragraphs discuss details; the last paragraph contains the closing.

CASE 8   THE POKER CHIP OUTLINE OF THIS BOOK

Cases 5, 6, and 7 have presented written messages which, although short, were poorly structured. The same principles used in developing a poker chip outline for these messages are equally appropriate and even more necessary for the longer message.

The structure of this book illustrates the use of the poker chip outline in a more complex message.

At the highest level, there are three parts to this book: (1) an opening which states the subject, explains its importance, and then previews the body of the book; (2) the body of the book; and (3) a closing which is essentially designed to answer the question, Where do I go from here?

The body of the book, describing the Behind the Words system, is divided into three blue chip headings of its own: People, Structure, Action. Under these three are the eight numbered red chip steps; and, in turn, under each red chip step are two or more white chip guides.

The sequence of poker chips at all levels in this book is usually a step-by-step sequence, because the book is explaining or instructing how to use a system. For example, the following are all arranged in step-by-step sequence: the blue chip headings—People, Structure, Action; the two red chip steps under Structure; and the three white chip guides under this Step 3. On the other hand, the red chip steps 6, 7, and 8 under the Action blue chip follow a functional sequence; each is concerned with a different subject (writing, reading, listening, and speaking).

Because the step-by-step sequence is used repeatedly in this book, it is preceded whenever possible by a point-first opening. For example, opening paragraphs at the beginning of each step help the reader orient himself and preview the step for him.

Step 4
Plan a Visible Structure

This step is the second red chip under the blue chip heading of Structure, and has three white chip guides:

- Avoid continuous narrative;
- Show meaning through word order;
- Follow the Clear River Test.

In the two People steps and in the first Structure step, the emphasis is on concepts and the structure of ideas. In this Step 4, the emphasis shifts to the structure of sentences and paragraphs. The three guides in this step will help you to plan a visible structure for your message, so that your message will be clearer to your audience. Although these guides apply primarily to the written word, they are also useful in oral presentations or face-to-face communications. (On page 130 is a section headed THE IF-THEN STRUCTURE OF RULES— of particular interest to those who write or analyze rules or systems of rules.) A summary of the guides follows:

AVOID CONTINUOUS NARRATIVE

Leave this to the novelist; it is seldom appropriate for business writing (or speaking). Use signposts freely. Plan a readable layout.

SHOW MEANING THROUGH WORD ORDER

Discard the bugaboos of traditional grammar; order is the key to the English sentence. (Included here is a discussion of the erroneous assumptions underlying every English grammar for 150 years and the change in approach reflected in the newer dictionaries.)

FOLLOW THE CLEAR RIVER TEST

Use this simple readability test to avoid creating unnecessary obstacles to readability.

AVOID CONTINUOUS NARRATIVE

Are You a Frustrated Novelist?

Novels, stories, magazine and newspaper articles, and many nonfiction books are typically written in a continuous narrative style, with longer paragraphs and sentences, no headings to break up the text or show the reader the way, and nothing other than the words themselves to show a change of emphasis or direction. Sometimes even the chapter headings mean little. This continuous narrative is appropriate for the novel, since the writer moves his story along paragraph by paragraph, chapter by chapter, working gradually toward his conclusion. Headings, other than at the highest level, would destroy the suspense and spoil the story.

Continuous narrative is often equally appropriate for magazine articles and general nonfiction books. In these cases, the writer does not usually have the purpose of motivating you to act his way but rather is writing to entertain, amuse, or inform you, or perhaps arouse other emotions. The writer's message is published in a general-circulation magazine or newspaper or in a book for sale to the general public. Those who buy and read it have no direct business relationship with the writer and therefore usually no need to study the message analytically to decide what action to take.

But all of this changes with the business message. Here the reader must read (or the listener must listen to) the message as part of his job. He must find within the message sufficient information so that he can decide what action, if any, he should take as a result of the message. Continuous narrative makes the reader's job difficult because it in adequately expresses the complex relationships between ideas and because it contains many conditional or qualifying clauses. To be sure he has missed nothing, the reader must consider every contingency and thus must read more material than is relevant to decide what is important and what is not. For these reasons, continuous narrative is particularly inappropriate (although widely used) in all forms of legal and technical writing.

The difficulty in understanding continuous prose is not caused entirely by the choice of words or by the meaning of individual clauses that make up the message; rather, it often arises from the lack of order in which ideas and sub-ideas are presented and the lack of clarity or visible structure in showing the relation of one idea to another. Affirmative, active, declarative sentences are the easiest to understand.

Also the continuous narrative style encourages long sentences and long paragraphs; again, this style may be satisfactory or even appropriate in the hands of a skillful storyteller who is weaving a spell or building suspense; but it is inappropriate, undesirable, and time-consuming in a business message, whether the message is written or spoken.

The business reader wants headings, labels, numbers, and other signposts that will identify for him the poker chip outline of the message, help him preview the message first so that he will know what to read carefully and what to skim, and stop him from wasting his time with ideas that he need not read.

Perhaps the business writer who inappropriately uses continuous narrative is a frustrated novelist; if so, the amount of unnecessary continuous narrative in business messages suggests that there are many frustrated novelists at large in business offices.

Use Signposts Freely

One simple way to break up continuous narrative is to use signposts freely. These include headings, numbers and letters, and a layout that shows the poker chip outline.

In a ten-page report, we would expect to find headings, probably numbered sections, and perhaps lettered sub-sections; but why confine this useful labeling of the poker chips to the long formal report? Why not use it also for the shorter letter, memo, or report and in your conversation or in an oral presentation?

If you are writing a three-page letter to a customer, and if in that letter you have two or more blue chip ideas, then, after your opening, use headings to let the customer know when you start discussing one idea and when you start discussing the next. The headings need be no more than a typewritten line by itself, in either all capital letters or initial capital letters (i.e., uppercase and lowercase) underlined. This simple device immediately shows the reader your poker chip outline and thus saves him the time of looking for it.

At the same time, these headings help you write a better letter. With the headings there, you are more likely to make cleaner transitions from one blue chip to the next, and you are less likely to include under one blue chip material that correctly belongs under another.

Yet how seldom do letters use simple headings such as this. Too often, the letter writer is following the style and format of the novelist in a situation where it is inappropriate.

For the longer written message, number and letter your headings. For example, number your blue chip headings;

letter your red chip headings. This is one more device to help the reader find his way and to help both you and the reader refer back to a particular part of the message.

Also for the longer written message, use layout as a signpost to show your audience the structure of the message. Secretarial handbooks and correspondence manuals generally contain satisfactory instructions for the layout of a typewritten letter, but they seldom adequately cover layout for the report or the more complex instruction; when they do, the suggested guides are not always well considered.

Here are four layout guides for complex single-column typewritten material, such as reports, proposals, briefs, instructions, etc.:

1. Use block margins throughout; move the margin to the right for subparagraphs.
    - Do not indent the first line of the paragraph beyond the margin to the remaining lines.
    - This principle avoids confusion and helps show the structure of ideas.
2. Limit the length of line to 65 characters.
    - The usual rule for length of line is stated in terms of the width of the left and right margins. This ignores the fact that typewriters using the smaller elite type have 12 characters to an inch; those with the larger pica type have 10 characters to an inch. Thus, 1-inch margins left and right produce a much more readable page with pica type than with elite type.
    - The 65 character limit is based on a rule of thumb well known to printers—the length of line should not exceed the width of $2\frac{1}{2}$ alphabets ($26 + 26 + 13 = 65$).
3. Single-space the final copy.
    - Double-spacing wastes white space by spreading it evenly between the lines. An effective layout uses white space to show structure.

- Double-space drafts, however, for ease of correction.
4. Include as detailed a table of contents as space permits.
    - This helps show the reader the structure of your message, makes reference to the message easy, and helps you as the writer to be sure your structure is sound.

The four guides above, and the lead-in sentence preceding them, have been set with block margins, as suggested in the first guide. By comparison, the same material follows, set first as a continuous narrative paragraph with no listing, and second with listing but without block margins. Compare the three visually and decide which is the more readable and which shows structure better.

(Continuous narrative)

Here are four layout guides for complex single-column typewritten material, such as reports, proposals, briefs, instructions, etc. First, use block margins throughout; move the margin to the right for subparagraphs. Do not indent the first line of the paragraph beyond the margin for the remaining lines. This principle avoids confusion and helps show the structure of ideas. Second, limit the length of line to 65 characters. The usual rule for length of line is stated in terms of the width of the left and right margins. This ignores the fact that typewriters using the smaller elite type have 12 characters to an inch; those with the larger pica type have 10 characters to an inch. Thus, 1-inch margins left and right produce a much more readable page with pica type than with elite type. The 65 character limit is based on a rule of thumb well known to printers—the length of line should not exceed the width of $2\frac{1}{2}$ alphabets ($26 + 26 + 13 = 65$). Third, single-space the final copy. Double-spacing wastes white space by spreading it evenly between the lines. An effective layout uses white space to show structure. Double-space drafts, however, for ease of correction. Fourth, include as detailed a table of contents as space permits. This helps show the reader the structure of your message, makes reference to the message easy, and helps you as the writer to be sure your structure is sound.

(Failure to use block margins)

Here are four layout guides for complex single-column typewritten material, such as reports, proposals, briefs, instructions, etc.

1. Use block margins throughout; move the margin to the right for subparagraphs.

   ▪ Do not indent the first line of the paragraph beyond the margin for the remaining lines. This principle avoids confusion and helps show the structure of ideas.

2. Limit the length of line to 65 characters.

   ▪ The usual rule for length of line is stated in terms of the width of the left and right margins. This ignores the fact that typewriters using the smaller elite type have 12 characters to an inch; those with the larger pica type have 10 characters to an inch. Thus 1-inch margins left and right produce a much more readable page with pica type than with elite type.

   ▪ The 65 character limit is based on a rule of thumb well known to printers—the length of line should not exceed the width of $2\frac{1}{2}$ alphabets ($26 + 26 + 13 = 65$).

3. Single-space the final copy.

   ▪ Double-spacing wastes white space by spreading it evenly between the lines. An effective layout uses white space to show structure.

   ▪ Double-space drafts, however, for ease of correction.

4. Include as detailed a table of contents as space permits.

   ▪ This helps show the reader the structure of your message, makes reference to the message easy, and helps you as the writer to be sure your structure is sound.

SHOW MEANING THROUGH WORD ORDER

The Bugaboos of Traditional Grammar

For over 150 years the teaching of English grammar in this country was (and, to some extent, still is) based on a seriously erroneous assumption, namely, that the rules of classical Latin grammar are appropriate for English grammar. This error was not widely challenged until the 1950s, following World War II and the experience of foreign language teaching in the armed forces during that war. Today far too many people still waste far too much of their and other people's time worrying about such irrelevant trivia as the flat prohibitions, common in all the traditional grammars, against splitting an infinitive or ending a sentence with a preposition.

The story of the error, a remarkable one, begins in seventeenth century England. The scholars of that time knew very little about their own language, but were well versed in the grammar of Latin and Greek. Latin grammar, for example, was taught to every schoolboy. These scholars mistakenly assumed that Latin grammar was not only the grammar of Latin, but that it was in some way a basic grammar appropriate for all languages and at all times. Had these scholars taken the time to study their own language, they soon would have realized that the grammar of English was not the grammar of Latin, but the scientific and inductive method of reasoning had not yet reached a point where this could be done. Also, these scholars felt that there was something noble and perfect about classical Latin (thus ignoring the point that Latin was a dead language). Thus, in developing an English grammar, they went to their Latin grammars without ever questioning the validity of their basic assumption.

Latin grammar did not apply to English then, and applies even less today. English was then and is increasingly more so today a distributive language, whereas classical Latin is an inflective language. This means that the two languages are radically different in the way that meanings are given to words and clauses.

For example, suppose you hear 2 five-year-old boys talking to each other. One of them says:

Him and me hates Tom.

By any standards, this sentence is grammatically wrong. To understand it, we need to convert it in our minds to a grammatically correct sentence that has meaning to us. There are two possibilities:

1. Tom hates him and me.
2. He and I hate Tom.

You and I instinctively convert the grammatically wrong sentence into sentence 2, not sentence 1. Yet, if we were to translate the original sentence from English into Latin exactly as it was spoken, we would have to use the singular verb form in translating "hates" and the accusative case of the pronoun in translating "him" and "me." Having done this, the only possible meaning for our sentence would be meaning 1 rather than meaning 2. In Latin, the inflections on the end of words determine their meaning; in English, the order in which the words are distributed in the sentence determines their meaning. Therefore when we see a pronoun or a verb in an English sentence that has the incorrect inflection (in this case, a singular verb where it should be plural and pronouns in the objective case where they should be in the subjective), we ignore the incorrect inflection and determine our meaning from the order of the words in the sentence. In a Latin sentence, the inflection is controlling, and the order of the words is disregarded.

This simple example illustrates the basic fallacy which lay behind the early English grammars. The first grammar of the English language was written (in Latin!) by John Wallis in the seventeenth century. He was followed in England by

Bishop Lowth and in this country by Lindley Murray, who published the first grammar here in 1795.

Murray's grammars, published in several editions over the years, were widely sold and widely copied. The rules of grammar that Murray stated as undeniable facts, not subject to question by anyone, came from Latin via Wallis's and Lowth's books, and in turn Murray's successors took them from him, still without question and without any attempt to determine whether these rules in fact were appropriate to the English language.

Murray's grammars and the grammars of those who copied him resemble a Latin grammar closely. The unfortunate student was required to learn by rote how to conjugate verbs in, for example, their active voice, indicative mode, and present, imperfect, perfect, pluperfect, first future, and second future tenses. Other modes included the imperative, potential, subjunctive, and infinitive. Some of Murray's imitators carried this approach to the ultimate, but logical, extreme of designing the grammar as a catechism. Here, for example, is an excerpt from a grammar written in 1830 for use in elementary schools in Connecticut, relating to the manner of parsing a noun.[4] The sentence to be parsed is "The boy plays." The questions and answers to be memorized were as follows:

Q. How do you parse boy?
A. Boy is a common noun, masculine gender, third person, singular number, nominative case to plays.
Q. Why is boy a noun?
A. The name of a thing.
Q. Why is it a common noun?
A. Because there are many.
Q. Why is it masculine gender?
A. The male kind.
Q. Why is it third person?
A. Spoken of.

[4] J. N. Dowd, *English Grammar*. Middletown, Conn.: Edwin T. Greenfield, 1830.

Q. Why is it singular number?
A. But one object.
Q. Why is it nominative case?
A. The agent of the verb.

Perhaps this deadly dull, sterile learning by rote of rules that were of no value in the day-to-day use of the language was not as difficult to students in the 1830s as it would be to us, since they learned many such similar rules by rote in Latin and in math; but what an appalling waste of time this process was, because the rules were not related to the English language as it is, but rather represented a misguided attempt to fit the language into the rules of Latin grammar. (Unfortunately, many remnants of this fundamental error are still apparent in teaching and usage today.)

In the 1950s, several books appeared which pointed out this basic fallacy, usually written by structural linguists who had approached the study of the English language from an entirely new direction. For example, Charlton Laird, in *"The Miracle of Language,"*[5] sums up the problem as follows:

> The root fact of English grammar is that English words have precise meaning in a certain position, and are gibberish in another position. This fact, however one wishes to phrase it, embodies the most important grammatical truth that can be enunciated about English: Order in the sentence is the basis of English grammar. And yet, barring a few students of Modern English, the chances are that not one in a hundred readers of this page will ever have heard anything like this statement before. That is the simple, the almost unbelievable truth.

Laird wrote that paragraph in 1953. A generation later, perhaps a few more than one in a hundred have heard this truth, but, unfortunately, still not very many.

[5] Reprinted by permission of The World Publishing Company, Cleveland, from THE MIRACLE OF LANGUAGE by Charlton Laird, p. 151. Copyright 1953 by Charlton Laird.

Part of the continuing problem may be that the linguists and grammarians of today, while in universal agreement that the old Latin-based grammars were wrong, are by no means in agreement as to what type of grammar should be used in the schools to replace them. Some linguists and psychologists ask whether grammar can really be taught at all. Robert A. Hall, in *"Linguistics and Your Language,"* makes this statement;[6]

> A six year old child has the basic sounds and grammatical patterns of his language down as well as he ever will have them, except for a few minor fluctuations that iron out soon afterwards.

The six-year-old child is ready to enter first grade. Hall is therefore saying that the six-year-old has already learned the basic sounds and grammatical patterns of his language as well as he ever will, although he can barely read or write. If you question Hall's statement, listen to a six-year-old-child. His sentences usually follow a standard subject-predicate order; also, he will usually, for example, connect a singular noun with a singular verb and use the subjective and objective cases of pronouns correctly.

This being so, then why study grammar in the early grades? The answer may well be that there is no point in doing so except for those fluctuations and exceptions that seem un-natural and must be learned from a book. A better time for this is sixth grade or later, not the early grades.

Even more surprising are the results of recent studies that show how the child of two or three has already learned, by a process that we cannot yet explain, how to discover abstract regularities of the language and to analyze at progressively deeper levels the sentences he hears so as to reproduce the

[6] By permission from Robert A. Hall, Jr., *Linguistics and Your Language.* Garden City, N.Y.: Doubleday & Company, Inc., Anchor Books, 1960, p. 34.

results in his own speech. It is not a simple process of imitation and correction.

A child of two, for example, will typically use the full form of "will" in declarative sentences although the child has not heard his mother use the full form this way. For example, the mother says, "We'll get it later," or "You'll ruin that." The child says, "I will get it," or "We will buy Mary a new one." The mother does, however, use the full form of "will" in questions, such as "Will it be fun?" In using the full form of "will" in the declarative sentence, the child is not imitating or copying his mother's sentences. The child's use of the full form of "will" in declarative sentences suggests that he has in some way analyzed the underlying "will" in his mother's contractive forms in these same declarative sentences. [7]

The validity of these studies can be tested by anyone who listens carefully to, and perhaps tape-records, the speech of a small child and his mother.

The purpose of this book is not, however, to explain the grammar of the English language. Rather, the purpose here is to explain the erroneous assumptions as to English grammar which prevailed without question in this country for 150 years and which still, to some extent, prevail today. The harm done is that they lead us to waste a lot of time emphasizing the wrong thing.

Ritual obedience to the positive, unexplained dos and don'ts of Murray's grammars dies hard in many people who were exposed to these rules at an early age, either at home or at school. Even if they reluctantly accept the fact that one of these rules has no grammatical validity, they then often continue to justify it on the grounds of personal taste, style, or usage. Thus, they consider it somehow inelegant or a sign of bad breeding if they split infinitives.

This leads directly to the question of who decides what is,

[7] By permission from Ursula Bellugi, "Learning the Language," *Psychology Today*. December 1970, p. 32.

or is not, proper usage—and that is the subject of the next section (where the split infinitive is also discussed further).

The New Look in Dictionaries

The new approach to grammar is reflected in a dramatic change in the underlying philosophy of dictionary editors. This is best illustrated by the change between *Webster's New International Dictionary*, second edition, first published in 1934, and *Webster's Third New International Dictionary*, first published in 1961.[8]

The second edition followed a prescriptive approach; the editors felt it was part of their job to tell their readers whether a particular usage was right or wrong. Twenty-seven years later, Philip B. Gove, the editor of the third edition, clearly influenced by the work of the structural linguists, took the approach that a dictionary's function is descriptive, not prescriptive. Language, like practically everything else, is in a state of constant flux so all a dictionary can do, he said, is to record how the language is being used in the year the dictionary is printed. Shocked by this change, traditional-minded reviewers panned the third edition when it first appeared. Yet, the underlying philosophy of the third edition seems inescapably correct—the English language (unlike Latin) is a living, growing language which cannot be frozen. Because a word is considered inelegant, vulgar, or colloquial in 1930 does not and should not mean that the word must always remain inelegant, vulgar, or colloquial.[9]

A classic example of this is the word "contact," used as a verb—as, for example, in the last sentence of a letter: "Please contact me if you have any questions." Webster's second edition lists this usage as "slang"; *Webster's New Collegiate*

[8] Published by G. & C. Merriam Co., Publishers of the Merriam-Webster Dictionaries.

[9] See Jack C. Gray, *Words, Words, and Words about Dictionaries*. San Francisco: Chandler Publishing Company, 1963.

Dictionary, 1949 edition, based on the second edition, moves it up one peg to "colloquial" with the warning that it is a "use avoided by careful writers and speakers"; Webster's third edition shows it as standard.[10]

The *Random House Dictionary*, another recent dictionary following the new approach, says this about "contact" as a verb:

> Many verbs in the English language are derived from nouns, and, grammatically at least, there is no justification for the criticism commonly heard of CONTACT used in these senses: *He contacted us about the shipments*. Despite the many objections of teachers and editors to this use on personal stylistic grounds, its currency is so widespread, simply because there is no other single verb in the language to express the same idea, that there is little doubt of its becoming universally acceptable in the future.[11]

The above quotation appears in one of the many usage notes in the *Random House Dictionary*. The editors of this dictionary take somewhat of a middle ground between Webster's second and third editions by recording their views of the current usage by educated people of certain disputed words and phrases.

Another new dictionary that carries this approach one step further is the *American Heritage Dictionary*. The editors of this dictionary asked a panel of 100 leading speakers and writers a wide range of questions as to their preferences, in the written and spoken language, concerning various disputed usages. This panel was concerned with literary English, not business English. Panel members expressed some scorn towards business English; a scorn justified when directed against gobbledygook but not justified when directed against

[10] By permission G. & C. Merriam Co., Springfield, Mass., op. cit.

[11] The Random House Dictionary of the English Language. Copyright 1971, 1969, 1967, 1966 by Random House, Inc. Reprinted by permission.

convenient new usages that help communicate ideas more efficiently. The dictionary records the percentage favoring the consensus of the panel.

In almost every case of a disputed usage, panel members are split. The conservatives shun it, the liberals see nothing wrong with it. For example, on the use of "contact" as a verb, 66 percent voted against it in formal contexts (but, again, this is literary English, not business English);[12] thus, 66 percent disagreed with the Random House usage note and with the Webster's third listing as standard.

Who is right? Who is wrong? Is it correct to use "contact" as a verb in a business letter? What about all the many other usages on which the American Heritage panel disagreed among themselves? Again, who is right and who is wrong?

The answer, obviously, is that in many cases there is no "correct" usage. Some writers, and some people, prefer to be more conservative than others in accepting the changes that are inevitable in a living language.

We need not criticize the conservative for resisting change when he does his own writing and thus keeps his preferences to himself; but when the conservative is a reviewer in a large organization who uses his editorial pencil to change other people's writing simply because their more liberal but still acceptable usages differ from his own, then he is wasting everyone's time and destroying the initiative of his subordinates.

- In working with federal agencies, where the review process is usually cumbersome, the author has several times found not only individual reviewers but sometimes entire divisions instructed that they must never split an infinitive. In one writing workshop, it became necessary to waste valuable workshop time to train partici-

[12] From the American Heritage Dictionary of the English Language, © Copyright 1969, 1970, 1971 by American Heritage Publishing Co., Inc. Reprinted by permission.

pants as to exactly what a split infinitive was, so that they could recognize it and therefore avoid it! Surely there were more important ways for letter writers in this agency to spend their time.

The test should be simply this—will my audience understand my message without any unnecessary waste, confusion, or delay? If the answer is yes, and if you do not violate any widely accepted standards of usage, then you are communicating efficiently.

An example of a convenient, useful, and grammatically correct usage that is not now and probably will never be accepted as standard English, either written or spoken, is the phrase "ain't I." The grammatically incorrect "aren't I" is more acceptable to educated listeners. Yet, "ain't I" is in fact a valid contraction of "am I not." (There is a limited exception here—in certain areas of the Deep South, "ain't I" is acceptable to well-educated listeners.)

Except for such obvious, well-known, and extreme examples as this, the business communicator should always ask himself whether a particular phrase or word communicates its meaning clearly and effectively to the audience. If it does, then he should use it, and anyone reviewing his work should avoid changes which simply substitute his own personal prejudices for that of the writer.

But, you may say, how about the reader? Suppose he is more conservative in his usages than I am. Should I not always follow the most conservative possible usage in every respect in order to avoid possible offense to some reader, particularly an important reader? The best answer here is that people are not reading your prose or listening to your statement to admire its polished perfection. They are reading or listening for meaning in order to know what action they should take. If the words and phrases used clearly convey that meaning, then the fact that your usages may be different from theirs will go unnoticed, particularly if your usage is one that many people, although perhaps not the majority, find acceptable.

Before closing this subject, let's look in more detail at the rationale for the prohibition against splitting an infinitive. From Wallis, Lowth, and Murray onward, it appeared in grammar after grammar without explanation. This prohibition apparently developed because in Latin and Greek (and many other languages) the infinitive is one word. Therefore, the so-called grammarians reasoned, in English the infinitive cannot be split. Once again, a fact of Latin grammar was incorrectly applied to English.

The usage note in the *Random House Dictionary* has this to say:

> The "rule" against splitting infinitives seems to have begun in the 17th century with John Dryden, who, in addition to being a famous dramatist, was a careful stylist and Latin scholar. In Latin, the infinitive is one word, hence cannot be split. Modeling English style on Latin style and grammar was then considered the epitome of good writing, so Dryden inveighed against the practice of using sentences like, *To really get to know someone you have to have lived with him.* But there is nothing inherent in English grammar or style to justify such an injunction, and, in a sentence like the preceding placing *really* anywhere else makes for awkward phrasing. Traditionalists', purists', and other schoolmarmish stylists' objections notwithstanding, there is nothing wrong with a split infinitive in English.[13]

In short, the decision as to whether or not to split an infinitive should be made on a basis of common sense—if the split infinitive gives the shade of meaning you want, or helps avoid an ambiguity, then by all means split it.

[13] By permission of Random House, Inc., op. cit.

Examples of Word Order Problems

This section contains a series of examples that illustrate the importance of sentence structure and word order in the English sentence.

1. Normal Word Order   The normal word order of a simple declarative English sentence is subject-predicate. The predicate consists of the verb and, if the verb is transitive, the object or, if the verb is intransitive, the word or words modifying the verb. Sometimes the object, or other verb modifier, is omitted; sometimes, the subject is omitted. But, to have a complete sentence, the verb can never be omitted; without a verb, there can be no sentence. (A skillful writer can effectively use sentence fragments without a verb; in such cases, the verb is implied.) Here are examples of simple declarative sentences:

The manager / phoned / the president.
Subject   Verb   Object

Eat / well.
Verb   Modifier

The bell / rang / loudly.
Subject   Verb   Modifier

The normal word order of subject-predicate is so firmly fixed in our minds that we can recognize it under unusual circumstances. Look at this example:

Gorbuk bronn frankishly crixling twinked the at the

Does that collection of nonsense words make any sense to you as you read it? Hopefully, it does not. Now let's rearrange the words as follows:

The crixling gorbuk twinked frankishly at the bronn.

Do these nonsense words now make some sense to you? The answer should be yes; although these words are nonsense, nonetheless we can begin to see the normal subject-predicate order in the sentence. "The crixling gorbuk" looks like the subject; "twinked" looks like a verb; "frankishly" looks like an adverb; and "at the bronn" looks like a prepositional phrase modifying the verb.

Now let's substitute some actual words for the rearranged nonsense sentence and read the two of them together:

The crixling gorbuk   twinked frankishly at the bronn.
The smiling foreman winked   happily   at the blonde.

The point here is that if you can see a normal subject-predicate order in this nonsense sentence, then this order is firmly fixed in your mind. When you want to communicate quickly and effectively, use this normal order instead of requiring your reader (or listener) to do the extra work of converting in his mind an unusual word order into the normal order.

Lewis Carroll's famous poem about the Jabberwock, with its opening lines:

Twas brillig, and the slithy toves

Did gyre and gimble in the wabe; . . .

is a classic example of nonsense words so cleverly arranged in a normal sentence order that the poem throughout appears to have real meaning.

Complex legal and technical sentences, particularly those with many conditional clauses, often fail to use a normal word order. The unfortunate reader must struggle hard to find his way through the sentence.

2. Word-order Ambiguity   As you leave the main offices of a factory in New England, this sign appears at an intersection at the end of the private road:

LEFT TURN ONLY FROM 4:30 TO 5:30 P.M.

This sign has two possible meanings, illustrating the ambiguities created by careless word order. The first meaning is that the only time of the day I may turn left is between 4:30 and 5:30; the rest of the day I can only turn right. The second (and intended) meaning is that I may turn left only, and therefore may not turn right, between 4:30 and 5:30. If in reading the sign you pause after the word "turn," then the sentence has the first meaning, but if you pause after the word "only," the sentence has the second meaning.

The adverb "only" is one of several that changes the meanings of sentences according to the position in which they appear in the sentence. Another example is the following:

Sentence	*Meaning*
1. Only he ate the fish.	No one else ate it.
2. He only ate the fish.	Ambiguous. Either the same meaning as sentence 1 or else the meaning of sentence 3, depending on where you pause in reading the sentence.
3. He ate only the fish.	He didn't eat anything else.
4. He ate the only fish.	There was only one fish.
5. He ate the fish only.	Same as sentence 3.

This example illustrates why efforts to avoid the split infinitive frequently result in serious ambiguities. For example, a contract contained the following clause:

The trustee shall require him promptly to repay the loan.

Does this mean that the trustee's action shall be prompt, presumably immediately following some other event, or does it mean that he must repay promptly? The second meaning seems more probable but, taken out of context, we cannot be sure. The ambiguity of word order here may well have resulted from one more effort to avoid splitting the infinitive. Assuming the second meaning was intended, this could have been unambiguously shown by splitting the infinitive:

The trustee shall require him to promptly repay the loan.

If the first meaning was intended, then the sentence should read:

The trustee shall promptly require him to repay the loan.

3. Point-first Sentence Structure   Step 3—Build a Poker Chip Outline—emphasized the advantages of a point-first sequence of ideas in the message as a whole. The same principle applies to the sequence of ideas in a sentence. Consider the main idea in a sentence as the blue chip in that sentence and the subordinate ideas, i.e., the modifying or conditional clauses, as the red chips. For the same reason that blue chips precede red chips in your overall outline, customarily write your sentences with the blue chip, or main idea, first, followed by the red chips, or secondary ideas. This is not an inflexible rule, but it is a sound and workable guide, particularly in business writing (or speaking).

For example, consider this opening clause in a sentence from a report:

Because of the results of the January survey showing over-crowding during existing hours and because of the almost unanimous opinions expressed by the supervisors, . . .

At this point you, the reader, having no idea what this clause modifies, are totally in the dark. Let's finish the sentence:

Because of the results of the January survey showing over-crowding during existing hours and because of the almost unanimous opinions expressed by supervisors, the committee recommended that the cafeteria remain open one-half hour longer.

Now the sentence makes sense. We can understand the red chip modifying clause when we know the basic blue chip idea of the sentence. In a sentence this short with only one modifying clause, the reader usually will not have forgotten or lost his grasp of the modifying clause by the time he gets to the main clause; therefore he will be able to understand the sentence on the first reading. But when several long, complex modifying clauses precede or surround the main idea, the reader quickly loses his way and, if he must understand the sentence, is forced to read it two or three times; more likely, if he is in a hurry, he simply goes on without being quite sure of the meaning of what he read.

As a manager or professional, you are not a novelist seeking to charm, excite, or amuse your audience by an unusual or interesting sentence structure. Your job is to communicate effectively and quickly; a normal sentence structure helps you do this, whether writing or speaking.

4. The Split-clause Ambiguity   Don't split a clause into two parts and scatter those two parts indiscriminately through the sentence. If you do, once again you are inviting ambiguity. For example:

In No. 2 warehouse, there are drums and tubas on the north side.

Are the drums on the north side? Probably they are because probably the writer intended to say:

On the north side of No. 2 warehouse, there are drums and tubas.

If he intended any other meaning, such as the tubas only were on the north side, then the sentence needs to be rewritten.

5. Check for Unity   Another guide in building a poker chip outline is to check for unity. Don't allow two ideas in any one unit. This applies not only at the outline level, but also at the sentence and paragraph level. For example, this sentence violates the principle of unity:

At present the 6,000-ton press is the only piece of heavy plate-forming equipment in the boiler shop, and it controls the capacity and the shipping schedules of this shop as the boiler drum is one of the first components shipped to the job site.

Although we can understand this sentence after perhaps the second reading, it is a clumsy sentence with at least two and probably three ideas in it. To help improve it, delete the "and," and substitute "because" for the weak "as." The sentence now reads as follows:

At present the 6,000-ton press is the only piece of heavy plate-forming equipment in the boiler shop. It controls the capacity and the shipping schedules of this shop because the boiler drum is one of the first components shipped to the job site.

These two sentences still need some further work but they are clearer now.

6. Ambiguities Are Lost in Continuous Narrative   Ambiguities can easily creep into continuous narrative. For example, when Hartford, Connecticut had its first ghetto riot in the 1960s, the mayor and the city manager, who had been quarreling for some time, each turned to the appropriate provision in the newly revised charter and each decided that this provision gave him the power to take the necessary action. The charter read as follows:

Whenever a public emergency exists . . . , the mayor may declare such emergency and summon the city manager to organize and direct the forces of every city department or agency in the needed service. He may summon, marshal, deputize, or otherwise employ other persons, or do whatever else he may deem necessary for the purpose of meeting the emergency. The city manager may obligate the city in an amount of money, not to exceed $100,000, to cope with such emergency until the council convenes.

The mayor said the "he" in the second sentence referred to the mayor; the city manager said it referred to the city manager. Clearly, the pronoun is ambiguous; the Corporation Counsel, after looking at the legislative history, decided it referred to the city manager.

Suppose that the provision had been structured as follows:

Whenever a public emergency exists . . . :
1. The mayor may declare such emergency and summon the city manager to organize and direct the forces of every city department or agency in the needed service.
2. He may summon, marshal, deputize or otherwise employ other persons, or do whatever else he may deem necessary for the purpose of meeting the emergency.
3. The city manager may obligate the city in an amount of money, not to exceed $100,000, to cope with such emergency until the council convenes.

The ambiguous pronoun "he" at the start of 2 now stands out like a sore thumb; the ambiguity would have been noticed early in the drafting process.

7. Step-by-Step Listing   The previous example showed how an ambiguity can be overlooked in a continuous narrative paragraph. The simple technique of step-by-step listing helped expose the ambiguity. This technique will often materially help you to reduce ambiguities in any written (or spoken) message and help make the message clearer to your audience.

Use step-by-step listing consistently whenever your message instructs someone to do, not to do, or how to do something, or whenever you are setting forth a sequence of ideas, whether in a sales letter, proposal, report, instruction, or for any other purpose.

For example, quoted below is the closing paragraph in a form letter used by an insurance company in sending a particular application form to policyholders. The letter was in use at the time that social security numbers first became widely used for general identification purposes and, hence, among other things, asks for the social security number. Here is the paragraph:

It is requested that the enclosed application for benefits be signed by you before a witness and dated. Also, the social security number of the person signing should be filled in on line 1. Before sending this form back to us in the enclosed self-addressed envelope, it is requested that the information included by us on this schedule be examined for correctness. If you should have any questions concerning this, please contact the undersigned.

This paragraph is a splendid example of rambling, stuffy, continuous narrative. Furthermore, most of the verbs are passive and impersonal. The various steps that the policyholder is required to take are not listed in a logical sequence; the writer forgot to tell the policyholder to have the witness sign the form. (People do as they are told in filling out forms; the insurance company received a surprising number of these applications without the witness's signature.)

Here is the same paragraph revised to include step-by-step listing:

Enclosed is your application for benefits. Please complete as follows:
  1. Fill in your social security number on line 1.
  2. Verify all information we have included on application and correct any that is wrong.
  3. Sign and date the application before a witness.
  4. Have the witness sign it.
  5. Return it to us in the enclosed envelope.
If you have any questions, please let us know.

Note that the five steps are now listed in a logical sequence, that each step begins with a verb, and that each step describes only one unit of action.

This use of step-by-step listing also avoids the ambiguous use of "should" in the original paragraph, second sentence. When the word "should" appears in an instruction, does it mean "may" or "must"? The use of "should" is common in instruction writing, perhaps because the writer wants to avoid the impression that he is giving his audience a peremptory order. Unfortunately it results in an ambiguity which people can and do take advantage of when they don't want to carry out the instruction. To avoid this problem, use step-by-step listing and start each item with a verb. This principle applies not only to a simple procedure such as this, but also to presenting or summarizing much more complicated ideas.

FOLLOW THE CLEAR RIVER TEST

Introduction

The Clear River Test is a simplified readability test that measures the number of words per sentence, words per punctuated pause, words per paragraph, and the number of syllables per hundred words. This test suggests as safe average scores for business and government writing the following:

- 25 words per sentence;
- 12 words per punctuated pause;
- 75 words per paragraph;
- 150 syllables per hundred words.

These scores are suggested because most writing in mass-circulation magazines and newspapers does not materially exceed these scores, on the average, and for some writing the scores are considerably lower. (As in golf, a low score is desirable on any readability test.) These scores therefore represent a comfortable reading level for most people.

Editors of mass-circulation magazines and newspapers

know from experience that their circulation will begin to drop off if they consistently print articles and stories written at a readability level too high for their audience. This does not mean that an editor takes the time to apply a readability test to a particular piece of writing that he suspects will score too high; from experience, he can judge this simply by looking at it.

The point of the Clear River Test (or of any readability test) is simply this: If a written message does not materially exceed the suggested safe limit for any of the four items, then the writer has placed no unnecessary obstacles between his audience and himself. But when a written message scores notably high in any one or more of these four items, the writer is placing unnecessary obstacles between the reader and himself. His message is written at a readability level higher than the level comfortable for most people. This means that he can expect his audience to have difficulty with his message; thus he faces the danger that his message will not get through, and therefore he will not accomplish his purpose.

The Clear River Test is not a precise mathematical test. In measuring readability, such a test would be burdensome to use and probably pointless. Rather, the Clear River Test provides a quick simple rule of thumb to help any writer or reviewer identify writing which is unnecessarily difficult and complex. The test therefore uses several shortcuts to make the counting less burdensome; with a little practice, a sample of writing can be tested in ten minutes.

The concept of the Clear River Test is shown graphically on the chart on page 120.

The four items to be scored are represented by concrete piers, with the suggested safe average scores placing these piers near the river's edge. The message is represented by a boat moving downstream from the sender to the receiver. As the scores for each item grow larger, the concrete pier rep-

CLEAR RIVER TEST

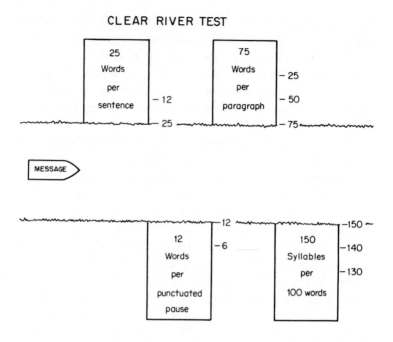

resenting that item must be built out further into the river, until finally the river becomes so obstructed that the message can no longer get through to its audience.

This test, designed primarily for business and government writing, is also useful for general nonfiction but is not intended to measure dialogue.

The suggested safe average river's edge scores are just exactly that. They are safe average scores, particularly for less-experienced and less-skillful writers, or for writers who lack the time or inclination to edit their copy vigorously.

A skillful professional writer who has the time to write and edit carefully may be able to handle long sentences and long paragraphs, and may be able to use relatively little punctuation, without producing writing that is difficult or clumsy. It has become currently fashionable in some popular magazines to write this way. The fashion seems a pointless one, but perhaps it is relatively harmless in magazines and articles written for general interest. In a business report written by a busy manager who is not a professional writer, this style slows down the reader and makes his comprehension more difficult.

The Clear River Test scores relate back to the building of a poker chip outline and to the planning of a visible structure. One of the principles of a poker chip outline, whether for the message as a whole or for a paragraph or a sentence, is to check for unity. This means that there should not be more than one idea or thought per sentence or paragraph. If your sentences on the average do not exceed twenty-five words, you will find it difficult to cram two unrelated ideas into one sentence; but if your sentences average seventy-five words, they can easily have more than one idea.

Also, unless you are a skillful writer with plenty of time, you will find that the blue chip and red chip ideas in a long sentence will probably not be clearly organized and thus your reader will be lost. Likewise if you keep your paragraphs short, you will avoid having too many ideas in one paragraph; if you use punctuation regularly, you give your reader a chance to pause and catch his breath.

The Clear River Test applies the People and Structure steps to the written word and, as the last guide under Structure, serves as a transition to Action—the last heading of the Behind the Words system. It applies the People steps because it recognizes that one of the answers to the third People Question—What do they want?—is always that the business reader wants writing that will be no more difficult than necessary for him to read and understand. Such writing will seldom have high readability scores.

Also, the test recognizes the need to catch and hold attention—a high readability score usually means difficult, boring writing. Finally, by encouraging short sentences and paragraphs, and sufficient punctuation, it encourages a visible poker chip structure for sentences and paragraphs.

In writing workshops for management groups conducted by the author's firm, thousands of participants have used the Clear River Test to compare the readability of their own on-the-job writing against the readability of mass-circulation newspapers and magazines. The suggested safe average river's edge scores, and the instructions for using the test (at the end of this guide), have therefore been proved by the actual experience of these workshops.

Other Readability Tests

The Clear River Test departs in three respects from previous readability tests: it is quicker to use, it measures two additional items, and it yields no composite score. The best known of these is probably Robert Gunning's Fog Index, which measures syllables per hundred words and words per sentence, using a carefully designed but complicated formula which Gunning now recognizes is more complicated than it need be. However, the Fog Index, at the time he first designed it, represented a substantial simplification of the very complex formulas originally developed.

The Fog Index was developed in the 1940s. At about the same time, Rudolf Flesch developed his "Reading Ease" and "Human Interest" scores. The Human Interest score is not applicable to business and government writing; it need not be considered further here. In the Reading Ease score, Flesch, like Gunning, counts the number of words per sentence and number of syllables per hundred words.

The Clear River Test scores two items not counted by Gunning or Flesch—words per paragraph and words per punctuated pause. The purpose of counting words per paragraph is to identify the writer who uses overly long paragraphs with too many ideas per paragraph. Counting words per punctuated pause helps identify the writer who does not use enough punctuation and thus requires his reader to take in too many words without a pause.

Gunning and Flesch both average their scores to produce a composite score which represents an overall reading level. A Fog Index of 12 on a particular piece of writing, for example, indicates that it is written at a twelfth-grade reading level. A Fog Index of 16 indicates a college-graduate reading level, etc.[14]

The Clear River Test does not produce a composite or average score. Rather, it shows whether a particular piece of writing is exceptionally high, and thus unreadable, on any one or more of the four items tested. If it is, then that piece of writing will usually be difficult for most readers, regardless of the scores on the other three items.

For example, a syllable count of 200 per 100 words virtually guarantees difficult writing; paragraphs that average 250 words each, sentences that average 100 words each, punctuated pauses that average 50 words each—any one of these, except in the hands of an unusually skillful and unhurried writer, will almost surely lead to confusing and weak structure and too many ideas per unit.

Instructions for Clear River Test

To use the Clear River Test, follow these instructions. Don't be discouraged by their apparent length—each instruction is explained carefully. With a little practice, you should be able

---

[14] See Rudolf Flesch, *The Art of Readable Writing.* New York: Harper & Brothers, 1949; Robert Gunning, *The Technique of Clear Writing.* New York: McGraw-Hill Book Company, Inc., rev. 1968; Robert Gunning, "The Fog Index After Twenty Years," *The Journal of Business Communication,* Winter 1968.

to score a piece of writing in ten minutes (substantially faster than other readability tests).

1. Choose your sample.
   - Do not use a sample full of numerals, abbreviations, proper names, or dialogue.
     - If possible, choose a sample with ten consecutive paragraphs having substantially the same length of line. Avoid a sample in which the length of line varies within the sample because of a photograph which cuts into a column (as in a magazine) or because of various levels of idented paragraphs, each level having a materially shorter length of line than the previous level.
     - If you must measure a sample where the length of lines vary substantially, count the paragraphs or subparagraphs with approximately the same length of line and ignore those that are not. If you cannot find ten consecutive paragraphs having substantially the same length of line, choose a smaller number of paragraphs or two or three groups of paragraphs that are reasonably typical, although not consecutive.
2. Mark the first word of your sample.
3. Count every word in the first ten full lines of your sample.
   - Do not count short lines at the end of a paragraph.
4. *Average words per line.* Divide your answer by ten, round it off to the nearest whole number, and write down the result.
   - This is the average number of words per line. You will use this in later steps.

- The use of this average is an important shortcut that saves tedious counting.

5. Count the first ten sentences of your sample; mark the last word of the tenth sentence.

   - Most sentences contain a complete thought, start with a capital letter, include a verb, and end with a period. These can be quickly counted; but there are some exceptions:

     - If a group of words represents a complete thought, including a verb, it is a sentence even though it may end in a semicolon, colon, or dash (or it may be surrounded by parentheses). Thus, immediately preceding the sentence you are now reading, the words in parentheses can be counted as a sentence; in the lead-in to this subparagraph, there are two sentences, one ending with a semicolon ("These can be quickly counted;") and one with a colon ("but there are some exceptions:").

     - In step-by-step listing, each subparagraph counts as a sentence, regardless of punctuation, if it is a complete thought standing by itself. It does not count as a sentence if the reader must go back to a verb some lines preceding in order to understand the complete thought.

     - If two complete thoughts are separated by a conjunction, such as "and" or "but," or are separated by a comma, count as one sentence only. A conjunction or comma is not a sufficient separation.

6. Count the number of lines in the first ten sentences.

   - Count short lines as fractions—i.e., if two lines at

the end of two paragraphs together equal a normal text line, then count as one full line. Note that this is different from Step 3, where you counted full lines only.

7. Multiply the number of lines in these first ten sentences by the average number of words per line (Step 4).
   - This gives you the estimated number of words in these ten sentences.

8. *Average words per sentence.* Divide your answer by ten and write down the result, rounded off to the nearest whole number.
   - This is the average number of words per sentence and is the first of the four scores you are seeking.

9. Count the number of punctuated pauses in the first ten sentences.
   - The purpose here is to count the number of punctuated pauses or points in a sentence where the reader may logically stop for a moment and catch his breath.
   - Count as one punctuated pause any punctuation mark following a word or group of words, except punctuation used to separate items in a series.
   - Count one punctuated pause for a sentence with no internal punctuation.

10. *Average words per punctuated pause.* Divide the estimated number of words in the first ten sentences (Step 7) by the number of punctuated pauses in these ten sentences. Write down the result, rounded off to the nearest whole number.
    - This is the average number of words per punctuated pause and is the second of the four scores you are seeking.

11. Count ten paragraphs in your sample; mark the last word of the last paragraph.

- A subparagraph counts as a paragraph if it contains at least one sentence.

12. Count the number of lines in the ten paragraphs.

   - Count short lines as fractions—i.e., if two lines at the end of two paragraphs together equal a normal text line, then count as one full line.

13. Multiply the number of lines in the ten paragraphs by the average number of words per line (Step 3).

   - This gives you the estimated number of words in the ten paragraphs.

14. *Average Words Per Paragraph.* Divide your answer by ten and write down the result, rounded off to the nearest whole number.

   - This is the average number of words per paragraph and is the third of the four scores you are seeking.

15. Count 100 words in your sample; mark the first and last word.

   - Avoid a sample full of numerals, abbreviations, proper names, or dialogue.

16. *Syllables Per 100 Words.* Count the number of syllables in the hundred words. Write down your answer.

   - To help the counting, pencil a mark on top of each syllable or after every five syllables.

   - In simplest terms, a syllable is a sound. In case of doubt, any good dictionary shows syllabication.

   - Government and business writing is frequently full of abbreviations for organizations. The syllable score would be distorted in a passage where polysyllabic names for government organizations or titles of people are constantly repeated. If you cannot avoid this type of sample for the syllable count, then count the abbreviations as you believe your audience would read them. This brings the syllable count down somewhat and seems reasonable. Some judgment is necessary here.

- For example, most readers would not pause long on the abbreviation "IBM" or "FBI." In a business report, it therefore seems reasonable to count either as one syllable, even though technically it should be counted as three, one for each letter.

- If your sample has many numerals, such as dollar amounts or quantities, use your judgment in deciding whether to *(a)* count each syllable, *(b)* count numerals as you believe the reader would read them, as in the "IBM" and "FBI" example, or *(c)* omit numerals entirely from the 100-word sample. Each of these alternatives leads to some distortion; hence, a sample with few numerals or abbreviations gives a more useful syllable count.

- If the item you are scoring includes necessary polysyllabic technical terms which the particular audience will clearly and quickly understand, a syllable count of up to 165 per 100 words is acceptable. But beware—necessary technical terms do not include unnecessary polysyllabic gobbledygook.

17. Enter your scores on the Clear River Test. How far out in the river do your piers go? Will your message get through?

A Quick Test for Readability   By applying the principles of the Clear River Test, you can quickly inspect typewritten pages for three of the four readability scores—average words per sentence, average words per paragraph, and average words per punctuated pause. Proceed as follows:

1. Assume an average of ten words per line.
   - For purpose of this quick test, this average is sufficiently accurate if your sample is typed with a standard pica typeface in a single column on a standard 8½-inch sheet, with the customary margins of about 1 inch on the left and right side of the pages. (Pica is the larger of the two standard typefaces on office typewriters; elite is the smaller.)
   - If your sample does not meet the usual standards listed above, or if you wish greater accuracy, count the number of words in the first ten lines and divide by ten (Steps 2, 3, and 4 of the Clear River Test, p. 124).
2. Inspect your typewritten pages. *On the average,* paragraphs should not exceed eight lines, sentences should not exceed three lines, punctuated pauses should occur at least every two lines.
   - Note that the above will give you a paragraph length of about eighty words, a sentence length of about thirty words, and a punctuated pause length of about twenty words. These are slightly higher than the recommended averages for the Clear River Test.
3. If you find a paragraph or sentence that materially exceeds the recommended line length, examine it carefully to see if it is too long and needs to be broken up.
4. If you find too many words per punctuated pause (i.e., too many words between punctuation marks), examine the sentence carefully to see if a comma or other punctuation mark is needed.

The quick test for readability described above is one that many experienced writers and editors use instinctively, as they review or edit their own or someone else's writing. It is simple to use and will quickly help you identify writing that obviously exceeds the standards of the Clear River Test.

There is no similar quick test for the syllable count per 100 words, the fourth of the four readability scores of the Clear River Test. However, if you will from time to time count syllables in 100 word samples from varying types of material, you will soon develop an ability to identify writing with an obviously too high syllable count.

THE IF-THEN STRUCTURE OF RULES

This section will be of particular interest to those who write or analyze rules or systems of rules — whether statutes, regulations, directives, orders, manuals, procedures, instructions, or any other set of rules.

The word "rule" as used here refers to a component part of any such set of rules.

The Rule on Rules

The IF-THEN structure of rules can be summed up in this little-known, little-understood, but vitally important rule on rules:

Every rule consists of a statement of one or more actions or results, preceded or followed by zero or more conditions.

This mathematically correct definition offers the key to the unwinding, restructuring, and analyzing of rules in a clear, sensible order.

The step-by-step listing example on page 117 shows an application of the rule on rules where there are no conditions, as is frequently true of procedures. The policyholder takes five steps to complete and return the form; each step constitutes a rule, without any conditions.

To illustrate the use of the rule on rules, this example shows a simple but badly written instruction made up of two actions, each subject to two conditions:

An employee who is eligible for overtime pay and works

more than forty hours in a work week, shall be paid over-time at the rate of time and a half, but those working more than forty hours who are not eligible for overtime pay will be credited with compensatory time.

When this sentence is unwound into its IF-THEN structure, it becomes two sentences and reads as follows:

An employee shall be paid overtime pay at the rate of time and a half, if:

1. He is eligible for such overtime; and
2. He works more than forty hours in a work week.

An employee shall be credited with compensatory time, if:

1. He is not eligible for overtime; and
2. He works more than forty hours in a work week.

The next example is a badly structured sentence from Section 402(b) of the Internal Revenue Code, (before the 1969 amendments) made up of one result subject to three conditions:

Contributions to an employees' trust made by an employer during a taxable year of the employer which ends within or with a taxable year of the trust for which the trust is not exempt from tax under section 501(a) shall be included in the gross income of an employee for the taxable year in which the contribution is made to the trust in the case of an employee whose beneficial interest in such contribution is non-forfeitable at the time the contribution is made.

Unwound into its basic IF-THEN structure, the sentence reads as follows:

Contributions to an employees' trust made by an employer shall be included in the gross income of an employee for the taxable year in which the contributions are made, if:

1. The employees' trust is not exempt from tax under section 501(a) in a particular taxable year of the trust; and

2. Contributions to the trust are made by the employer during a taxable year of the employer which ends within or with such taxable year of the trust; and

3. The beneficial interest of the employee in such contributions is nonforfeitable at the time the contributions are made.

Note that the identical words are used in the revision, except that for clarity sufficient words have been repeated in each condition to make it a complete sentence.

The first of the two examples above is from a clerical procedure; the second is from tax law. Yet each is written in a rambling, continuous narrative style with no awareness of its basic IF-THEN structure. Similar examples can be found everywhere, in every kind of set of rules. The Internal Revenue Code has many other sentences far worse than the short example quoted above [the over 400-word nonstop sentence in Section 341(e) is notorious]; insurance policies are full of long and unbelievably complex sentences that totally ignore the IF-THEN structure of the rules they are stating; operating rules and procedures frequently mix conditions and actions so thoroughly in the same sentence that the user can easily become very confused.

The process of breaking down a messy set of rules into its inherent IF-THEN structure can best be understood by a step-by-step analysis of the before-and-after examples shown above. Once you understand the process in these examples, then you will find you can apply it without difficulty to longer and more complex material. It takes time to unwind a thoroughly snarled set of rules, but the process is not difficult, once you understand it.

First, find and underline the main subject, main verb, and main object, if any, in the sentence. This is the blue chip action, or result; if there are two or more blue chips, underline each.

In the overtime example, the skeleton blue chip ideas consist of these words: "An employee . . . shall be paid overtime," and ". . . those [i.e., employees] . . . will be credited with compensatory time."

In the tax example, the skeleton blue chip idea is: "Contributions shall be included in the gross income. . . ."

Next, find and underline the conditions for each rule. Again, identify only key words.

In the overtime example, the key words for the two conditions relating to the first rule are: ". . . who is eligible . . ." and ". . . works more than forty hours. . . ."

The key words for the conditions relating to the second rule are ". . . working more than forty hours . . ." and ". . . who are not eligible. . . ."

In the tax example, the key words for the three conditions are ". . . taxable year . . . for which trust is not exempt . . . ," "[Contributions] . . . made . . . during taxable year . . . trust is not exempt," and ". . . beneficial interest . . . non-forfeitable. . . ." Finding and isolating the three conditions is difficult in this example; in a misguided effort to save words, the draftsman has constructed a nonstop eighty-three-word sentence with no punctuation, a sentence in which conditions and results are thoroughly and unnecessarily snarled.

As you study the unwinding of these two examples, note that in each case the main subject and main verb are separated by one or more conditions. This is a sure way to confuse the reader.

The action, or result, is the blue chip; always state it first in full, followed by the key word "if"; then state the red chip conditions as full sentences in step-by-step order. This applies the point-first sequence at the sentence level; red chip conditions are always subordinate to the blue chip action, or result.

Do not use "when," "where," or "in the event that" as synonyms for "if"; the first two can be ambiguous ("when" has a time meaning, "where" has a place meaning) and the third is a wordy, pompous substitute. The little two-letter word "if" unequivocally and unambiguously tells the reader a condition is to follow.

Do not start the sentence with "if," if you are drafting a complex rule; most of the truly monstrous sentences in statutes, regulations, and insurance policies start with "if." You are putting the cart before the horse when you start with "if," because conditions are red chips; results are blue chips. The complex rule that starts with "if" becomes particularly difficult to understand if there are conditions and subconditions within the same rule—i.e., some conditions are cumulative, and others are alternative. A step-by-step listing visually sorts out the cumulative ("and") conditions from the alternative ("or") conditions; the latter should always be shown as subordinate to the former and should be indented one level further to the right of the page.

Decision Tables: a Tool for Analysis

When the rule or set of rules you are working with is complex and full of conditions, use a decision table as a tool for analysis.

The decison table (also called "decision logic table") offers you a simple way of arranging a detailed narrative statement of IF-THEN relationships in a chart or table format to help you select more quickly the information you want. One part of the table describes the circumstances or conditions that exist (the IFs), and the other outlines the action required or result necessarily following for each set of circumstances or conditions (the THENs).

The reader of a completed decision table need only find the circumstances or conditions which apply to his particular situation and take the appropriate action to know that the appropriate result will follow. In other words, to make a decision, establish the conditions (the IFs) that will dictate the actions or results (the THENs). All decisions represent an IF-THEN sequence.

Decision tables are widely used by computer programmers where conditions are complex because the tables represent a substantial improvement over either the flow chart or a narrative. The decision table is useful also in any problem-solving process, because it charts the fundamental IF-THEN structure of thinking. Neither of these uses will be considered here.

Both the Army and the Air Force have revised certain of their regulation systems from a series of narrative paragraphs to a series of decision tables, with narrative entirely eliminated, except for explanatory opening sentences and an occasional footnote.[15] In general, users have found the decision-table format a distinct improvement over the narrative-paragraph format.

The form of decision table used in Army and Air Force regulations is the horizontal extended entry. Here is how the overtime pay instruction reads, in this form of decision table (without the use of any shortcuts or abbreviations):

IF	AND IF	THEN
1. Employee is eligible for overtime	Employee works more than 40 hours in work week	Pay overtime at time and a half
2. Employee is not eligible for overtime	Employee works more than 40 hours in work week	Credit with compensatory time

In the above table, read the rules from left to right. For example, IF employee is eligible for overtime, AND IF em-

---

[15] See AFP 5-1 (Air Force) and TAGO 7809A (Army), *The Decision Logic Table Technique*. Also see Herman McDaniel, *An Introduction to Decision Logic Tables*. New York: John Wiley & Sons, Inc., 1968.

ployee works more than forty hours in work week, THEN pay overtime at time and a half.

In setting up a decision table, the convention is to state the conditions first. There are probably two reasons for this: one is historical; the other is practical.

Historically, decision tables are an outgrowth and application of symbolic logic, in which it is standard to state the conditions first. For practicality, most users enter the table knowing a particular set of facts or circumstances for which they are seeking the appropriate action or result. In reading from left to right, it is easier to start with the known conditions and proceed to find the wanted action or result. The problems (referred to in the previous section) caused by starting a sentence with "if" are not present in the decision-table format.

You are free to construct a decision table in any format that you find useful, if you are preparing the table only for your own analysis and convenience.

Another widely used format is the vertical limited entry. In this format, the overtime pay instruction would read as follows:

	IF	1	2
A.	Employee is eligible for overtime	Y	N
B.	Employee works more than 40 hours in work week	Y	Y
	THEN		
C.	Pay overtime at time and a half	X	
D.	Credit with compensatory time		X

"Y" means yes; "N" means no; "X" means the indicated action or result applies.

In the above table, read the first rule down the page as follows: "IF employee is eligible for overtime—Yes, he is; IF employee works more than forty hours in work week—Yes, he does; THEN pay overtime at time and a half." Sometimes the conditions are easier to understand if worded as questions—i.e., "Is employee eligible for overtime?"

The vertical-limited-entry format takes a little practice at first to become accustomed to reading down rather than across and to supply the appropriate yes and no answers. It has the great advantage over the horizontal-extended-entry format of allowing the table to be constructed on an ordinary sheet of ruled paper and of allowing many conditions and results to be covered on one page. For purposes of analysis, such a one-page table or chart is invaluable.

It is beyond the scope of this book to provide detailed instructions for constructing decision tables. The following five guides should be sufficient, however, along with the two previous examples and the longer one that follows, to show you how to construct a simple table for your own use:

1. Limit each IF statement to one single fact or circumstance.
2. Limit each THEN statement to one single action or result.
3. Use key words only in describing the IFs or THENs; don't clutter your table with unnecessary words.
4. If a particular item can be placed under either an IF or a THEN heading (this often happens), place it under the IF heading.
5. Write a new rule for each alternative IF and each alternative THEN.

The fifth guide above states one of the real advantages of the decision table; you cannot, in the same rule, combine alternative and cumulative IFs or THENs. All IFs in one rule and all THENs in one rule must be cumulative; otherwise you do not have one, single unambiguous rule.

For example, this states a rule: If A is so AND B is so, then X is so AND Y is so. This states two rules: If A is so OR if B is so, then X is so AND Y is so. This does not state a rule: If A is so AND if B is so, then X is so OR Y is so. In the first case, if the two conditions exist, the two results must inevitably follow. In the second case, either condition produces two results. In the third case, the result is unpredictable and therefore cannot be stated in decision-table form.

The final example in this section, included for those who want to see the use of a decision table to unwind a highly complex sentence, presents a sentence that once appeared in the *Federal Register*. It concerns regulations of the Food and Drug Administration and is a classic illustration of a non-stop sentence (221 words), in which the IFs and THENs are scrambled together in an absurdly and unnecessarily complex pattern. The decision tables following the sentence show its basic IF-THEN structure; for convenience, the tables are presented in both formats.

If you study this example carefully, you may well decide that you could have constructed the table differently in some details. This indicates simply that in analyzing a complex written set of rules, there is more than one correct way of setting up the table. Also, a full knowledge of all the underlying facts could lead to a somewhat different table. However, the tables shown represent an accurate picture of the basic IF-THEN structure of this sentence, as it appears, without benefit of any background information.

The sentence is as follows:

(e) If the Commissioner finds that new evidence of clinical experience or other information regarding the safety or effectiveness of a drug listed in Sec. 103.302(b) invalidates a prior conclusion that a drug is generally recognized by qualified experts as safe and effective for use under the conditions set forth in such a regulation, he shall:

(1) After furnishing public notice of the proposal in the FEDERAL REGISTER and opportunity for comment thereon:

(i) Promulgate a revision of the conditions set forth in

the regulation to establish conditions under which he finds
that the drug is generally recognized by qualified experts
as safe and effective; or

(ii) Promulgate an order revoking such listing of the
drug when he finds that the drug has not been used to a
material extent or for a material time under conditions of
use that are generally recognized by qualified experts as
safe and effective; or

(2) Promulgate an order immediately revoking such listing of the drug if:

REVISION OR REVOCATION OF DRUG LISTING

RULE	IF	AND IF	AND IF	AND IF	THEN, COMMIS-SIONER SHALL
1.	New evidence . . . invalidates prior conclusion	Public notice			Revise conditions
2.			Nonmaterial use		Revoke listing
3.			Imminent hazard	Secty. suspended approval	Revoke listing immediately
4.				No approval	

	IF	1	2	3	4
A.	New evidence . . .	Y	Y	Y	Y
B.	Public notice . . .	Y	Y	N	N
C.	Nonmaterial use . . .	N	Y	N	N
D.	Imminent hazard . . .	N	N	Y	Y
E.	Secty. suspends approval	N	N	Y	N
F.	No approval in effect	N	N	N	Y
	THEN				
G.	Comm. shall revise conditions	X			
H.	Comm. shall revoke listing		X		
I.	Comm. shall revoke listing immediately			X	X

(i) The Secretary has suspended the approval of a new-drug application for such drug immediately on a finding that there is an imminent hazard to the public health, as provided in section 505(e) of the act; or

(ii) The Commissioner finds that there is an imminent hazard to the public health and that no approval of a new-drug application is in effect for such drug.

The use of a decision table (either format) quickly shows the basic IF-THEN structure of this 221-word sentence, which actually contains four rules. The table also suggests an outline to use in rewriting this sentence in simpler, clearer language:

1. The first paragraph of the revision would create a defined term "new evidence" (or a similar phrase) to cover the common condition now appearing in the first clause of the original, down to the first comma. Next would follow four separate paragraphs, each stating one rule, outlined as follows:

2. Commissioner shall revoke listing immediately of listed drug, if
   A. He finds "new evidence," and
   B. He finds imminent hazard, and
   C. No approval of new-drug application is in effect.

3. Commissioner shall revoke listing immediately of listed drug, if
   A. He finds "new evidence," and
   B. He finds imminent hazard, and
   C. Secretary has suspended approval.

4. Commissioner shall revoke listing of listed drug, if
   A. He finds "new evidence," and
   B. He complies with public-notice requirements, and
   C. He finds nonmaterial use.

5. Commissioner shall revise conditions, if
   A. He finds "new evidence," and
   B. He complies with public-notice requirements.

Note that the above outline is exactly that—an outline from which the revised version of the sentence could be rewritten.

The purpose of this section has been to call attention to the IF-THEN structure of rules and to show how a simple decision table can be a useful tool for analysis of complex rules. If more rule-writers understood the IF-THEN structure, the extraordinarily complex and badly structured sentences so often found in rules could gradually be eliminated.

If your work requires you to analyze or write complex sets of rules, you will find it well worthwhile to study this section carefully. Your ability to recognize IF-THEN structures will save you time and help you to do a better job.

THE BEHIND THE WORDS SYSTEM

Part 3
Action

*The final blue chip heading of the Behind the
Words system, and thus the base of the Behind
the Words triangle, is Action. Under this heading
are collected the key steps and guides concerning
the act of communicating. The Action heading has
four red chip steps:*
  Step 5. Follow the Brisleditch Guides
  Step 6. Write Effectively
  Step 7. Read Effectively
  Step 8. Listen and Speak Effectively

Step 5
Follow the BRISLEDITCH Guides

The basic principles for using words well may be conveniently grouped under these five guides:

Be <u>bri</u>ef
Be <u>simple</u>
Be <u>direct</u>
Be <u>c</u>lear
Be <u>h</u>uman

The underlined letters spell the acronym BRISLEDITCH (pronounce it "Bristle Ditch").

The BRISTLEDITCH guides help you choose the right words, whether you are writing or speaking.

For the most part, these guides do not represent new principles; rather, at this point they are reminders to help you apply the guides already developed under the People and Structure steps. Each of the BRISLEDITCH guides therefore relates back to one or more principles already discussed.

The cumulative effect of the Behind the Words approach presented in this book can be seen at this point. If you have asked yourself the People Questions and answered them intelligently, if you have considered how you can use motivators and chosen the appropriate ones, if you have built a sound poker chip outline and planned a visible structure, then the problems of choosing words well become much simpler, particularly in a business communication.

The skilled novelist may spend much time in choosing exactly the right word to reflect his personal style and convey the shade of meaning he desires. He may edit and reedit so that every word in his story is exactly the word he wants to use.

In business and government communications, we seldom have either the time or the need to do this. Our audience is reading not to admire the polished perfection of our prose but, rather, for meaning; to find out what action, if any, they should take as a result of our message. (This is one of the points mentioned in the introduction that distinguishes management communications from writing generally.) If we communicate clearly and efficiently, then it is not always essential that we have chosen precisely the right word, as long as the word we have chosen conveys its meaning clearly. Of course, certain key words in some messages must be chosen carefully.

The five BRISLEDITCH guides are not rules. If you follow these guides consistently as you choose your words, your writing and your speaking will be more effective; but exceptions are always appropriate. For example, if you want to be courteous, avoid being too brief, too simple, too direct, or even too clear. Likewise, never be brief at the expense of being clear; the extra words that help make your meaning clear to your audience are usually words well worth using.

The BRISLEDITCH guides often overlap each other so that a particular problem in the use of words may fall under more than one guide. In the following discussion, however, each guide is considered separately.

The first three guides — Be brief, Be simple, Be direct — represent the basic and essential editorial steps that every good writer follows when he takes out his pencil to edit his own writing. As speakers, these guides help us edit our words before we speak. The last two steps — Be clear, Be human — bring you directly back to your audience. Be clear not just to yourself or your associates but also to all your audience. Be human because people communicate with people; your audience consists of people like yourself, not numbers in a computer.

BE BRIEF

Cut out unnecessary words.

Most business writing contains more words than are necessary; drastic pruning will almost invariably improve it. Sometimes these words can be removed without any loss of meaning at all. In other cases, one or two words can be substituted for many words.

Professional writers, in describing the editing process, invariably emphasize the importance of vigorous pruning. For example, Peter de Vries has said, "Revision is mostly compression — frying the fat out of it, I call it. When I see a paragraph shrinking under my eyes like a strip of bacon in a skillet, I know I'm on the right track. . . ."[16]

Three examples of sentences that badly need pruning will suffice here to make the point (many others can be easily found):

1. This is from the report of a claims representative of an insurance company:

---

[16] Peter de Vries, "de Vries on Rewriting in the Supermarket," LIFE Magazine, December 17, 1968 © Time, Inc.

During the recent storm in Topeka, a helicopter was in the course of inspecting the various damaged areas when, for some unknown reason at this time, the helicopter crashed causing the loss of life to the pilot, Peter C. Petroski.

After the obvious pruning, this sentence reads as follows:

During the recent storm in Topeka, a helicopter was inspecting the damaged areas when, for some unknown reason, it crashed killing the pilot, Peter C. Petroski.

The careful writer would note that the pilot and not the helicopter was doing the inspecting. However, the meaning is clear and the real problem with the sentence is too many useless words.

2. Here is another example, from a letter to a customer:

We wish to acknowledge your letter of October 27 and in reply wish to state that the item you inquired about was mailed yesterday.

Pruning here gives us the following:

Thank you for your letter of October 27. The item you inquired about was mailed yesterday.

3. Here is another one:

We are in a position to begin work on this job as soon as we are authorized to do so. We will contact you next week with respect to such authorization.

After pruning, this one becomes:

We can begin work on this job as soon as you authorize us. We will contact you next week regarding authorization.

The editorial changes required on the above three examples primarily involve crossing out unnecessary words and substituting a few words for many. These changes also lead to eliminating unnecessary polysyllables, and this brings us to the next guide—Be simple.

But first, why is brevity desirable?

The answer to this brings us right back to the People Questions in Step 1. The first question asks—what is your purpose? In a business communication, your purpose is to communicate efficiently and clearly to your audience so that they will understand your message without unnecessary waste, confusion, misunderstanding, or delay and therefore will be able to act on it in your way (if they so choose).

One of the general answers to the second People Question— Who is involved?—is that you are communicating with busy people who do not want to spend any more time reading your communication or listening to your message than is absolutely necessary.

The third question—What do they want?—again reminds you that these busy people, because they do not want to waste any time on your message, want it to be as brief as possible. The briefer it is, the less time they will need to read it, the more likely they are to read it all the way through, and thus the more likely you are to achieve your purpose.

Finally, one sure way to catch and hold attention is to keep your message brief; one sure way to lose the attention of your audience is to be wordy.

BE SIMPLE

Avoid gobbledygook and pompous polysyllables.

By far the most common disease in business and government writing is the deadly overuse of gobbledygook and pompous polysyllables. (The expressive word "gobbledygook" was coined by Congressman Maury Maverick during World War II, after he became particularly fed up one day with the polysyllabic verbosity of government reports.) Unfortunately, we all laugh, despair, or become irritated at the other man's gobbledygook, but too often we fail to recognize our own.

If you have a large vocabulary, don't use it when you write or speak; never use a large word if you can use a small one. Schools make a serious mistake in urging students to look up big words in a thesaurus and substitute them for simple, everyday words. Save your large vocabulary for your reading or listening.

Why is gobbledygook bad? Why should you avoid pompous polysyllables? Quite simply, this kind of language does not help you communicate your message clearly and usually is deadly boring to read.

Gobbledygook always has a high syllable count. If you consistently write with polysyllables, your writing will be well beyond the river's edge score of 150 syllables per 100 words suggested by the Clear River Test.

Sometimes writers in the lower or middle level of an organization, preparing a report for senior people, will deliberately use big words because they believe that senior people are impressed by these words. (This is "writing to impress" rather than "writing to express".) People who make this serious mistake, and it is always a serious mistake, fail to realize that the top men, who seldom use polysyllables themselves (generally people at the top are effective communicators), are busy and resent being required to waste time extracting the meaning from these polysyllables. The writer, rather than impressing the audience with these big words, risks depressing them to the point where they will think less rather than more of him because of his choice of big words.

Not all big words represent gobbledygook or pompous polysyllables. Sometimes a polysyllabic technical word has been coined because it precisely describes something and there is no other one word or perhaps even combination of words that describes it so precisely. Necessary technical words may be used cautiously if the writer is sure that everyone in his audience will understand them. If he is not sure, and if he must nonetheless use these words, then he should carefully define them.

Several examples of a failure to be simple follow.

1. Here is a typical example of administrative pomposity:

> Division managers are herewith requested to facilitate the implementation of the aforementioned program by forwarding to this office at their earliest convenience copies in quadruplicate of their personnel requirements during the forthcoming calendar quarter.

After the necessary pruning, this miserable sentence reads as follows:

> Division managers are asked to help carry out this program by sending to this office as soon as convenient four copies of their personnel requirements for the next quarter.

2. Instructions can sometimes be so obscured by gobbledygook that their main point is missed. For example, this appeared on a piece of equipment at Cape Kennedy:

> Warning: The batteries in this unit could be a lethal source of electrical power under certain conditions.

An unknown serviceman translated this gobbledygook into everyday English and, impressed by the seriousness of the message, wrote this in pencil underneath the sign:

> Look out! These batteries could kill you.

3. Here is another example of administrative pomposity:

> This procedure is designed to facilitate the expeditious movement of cargo with a minimum of documentation. There should be no inference that commodities accommodated by this procedure would or will receive priority treatment over normal transactions.

After translation, those two sentences say no more than this:

This procedure is designed to help move cargo faster with a minimum of documents. The cargo moved under this procedure will not, however, receive priority over normal transactions.

4. This sentence is from a consultant's report to senior management:

If the company were able to effect a reduction in the cost of its raw material purchases to the price of $1.23 per pound appearing in the engineering report, the effect upon the company's income statement would be substantial.

Cut down to size, it reads as follows:

If the company could buy its raw materials for the $1.23-per-pound price shown in the engineering report, the company's income would be substantially improved.

Notice the vagueness in the last clause of the original example 4—a typical result of the use of gobbledygook. The writer does not tell you whether the company's income statement would be improved or hurt. Furthermore, it is not the effect on the statement that is important, it is the effect on the income. Also note in the original the clumsy use of the word "effect" twice in the same sentence to express two different meanings. In each case, the word is unnecessary.

5. The problems of gobbledygook are not limited to businessmen and government agencies. They are endemic whenever any group of managers or professionals work together in a particular area. Thus, gobbledygook and jargon are frequently closely connected. Jargon problems belong under both "Be simple" and "Be clear." For example, these sentences are from a speech by a distinguished psychiatrist to a group of laymen:

As to the interpersonal difficulties that arise, these are as often the result of deficiencies in communication as of disorders in personality. Employee and employer, coworker and supervisor, subordinate and superordinate form an interlocking system in which there can be much displacement and aggravation of personality and situational problems. At times, hostilities are displaced and rancors inflated to an enormous degree.

The psychiatrist making his speech was sincerely attempting to get across an important message to a group of laymen. How many laymen in his audience understood what he was talking about? How many laymen (or even fellow psychiatrists) had ever heard the word "superordinate"?

Let's try to translate this:

> Conflicts between people are caused as often by communications problems as they are by personality disorders. Superiors and subordinates in an organization form an interlocking system in which many serious personality and situational problems arise.

Perhaps there is more in those sentences than the revised version suggests, but, if so, the pompous polysyllables and in-house jargon have thoroughly obscured the message.

The list is endless. Engineers, lawyers, psychiatrists, educators, professors; each group develops its own polysyllabic in-house jargon. To understand the terms, you must be a member of the group, and even then, you may not be sure.

Why do people write this way? Is it laziness? To some extent, yes. A vague, polysyllabic term is often a substitute for clear thought. Also, the writer somehow feels that by using words unfamiliar to his reader, he makes his own job and his own status more important. Lawyers are often accused of using big words to create more work for themselves and to mystify their clients. But it isn't just lawyers who do this, as the next example shows.

6. This hideous specimen is written by a systems analyst in a large aerospace corporation:

> The implementation of this program will stimulate intercomponent consultation in all phases of systems development and will focus intercomponent discussion at critical decision points. Success will depend, in great measure, on the broad and mutual communication of sound documentation and approved system plans. Only by the introduction of an appropriate degree of order and flexibility into the development process can the most prudent judgments on priorities be agreed upon.

If there is any meaning at all in the above paragraph (and this is questionable), it is probably along these lines:

> This program will encourage intercompany meetings on systems development and will focus discussion in these meetings on key decision points. Success will depend on effective communication. As the program is developed, both order and flexibility will be required.

A paragraph as polysyllabic and confused as the uncorrected example seriously reflects upon the competence of its author, first, because it is far from clear whether he had anything important to say, and, second, because the writer obviously has not thought through his message clearly and is simply substituting in-house jargon and gobbledygook for clear thought.

BE DIRECT

Use strong, active verbs and a normal sentence order. The importance of using a normal sentence order is fully illustrated in Step 4—Plan a Visible Structure; examples of the problems caused by poor word and clause order need not be repeated here. The admonition to use a normal sentence order is repeated as a part of the Be direct guide, however, because we can check for normal sentence order as we choose or edit the words we use.

Be direct also warns us to use strong, active verbs. This important principle is discussed in detail at this point.

The active voice is more direct, more powerful, more effective, and avoids confusion as to the actor's identity. The passive voice is greatly overworked in business and government writing; a fair estimate would be that it is used 80 percent of the time when it would be appropriate to use it 40 percent of the time.

In the active voice, the subject does something to the object (if the verb is transitive), or the subject does something (if the verb is intransitive).

  1. For example:

      1A. Active transitive: The dog bit the man.
      1B. Active intransitive: The dog ran.

The first of these examples is turned into the passive as follows:

      1C. The man was bitten by the dog.

Frequently, when the passive is used, the name of the actor is omitted:

      1D. The man was bitten.

Transposing a sentence from the active to the passive usually results in a few extra words and in a less-powerful sentence. The meaning is equally clear as long as the name of the actor is included, as it is in 1C.

The passive would be appropriate in this case to emphasize that the man and not, for example, the woman was bitten by the dog. The passive is also correctly used if the writer or speaker wants to emphasize the person or thing acted upon.

If the name of the actor is omitted, as in 1D, then ambiguity can and frequently does occur. In this case, what was the man bitten by—a dog, a bee, a snake? Consistent use of the active avoids the ambiguity of not knowing who the actor is.

If it is unimportant to state the actor, then the use of the passive is correct. For example, in the lead-in clause to example 1C, the verb phrase "is turned into" is a passive with the name of the actor omitted. The same clause with the name of the actor supplied would produce this awkward result: "The reader can turn the first of these examples into the passive as follows":

2. This example of an unnecessary and clumsy passive also illustrates the weak-verb problem:

> 2A. No contact has been made by either Mrs. Smith or her attorney with the bank.

Changing the passive into active produces the following sentence:

> 2B. Neither Mrs. Smith nor her attorney has made contact with the bank.

The verb "made" in 2A has no meaning by itself and thus is weak. The key word in the sentence is the noun "contact." Turn this noun into a verb, shift to the active voice, and you have the following shorter and more powerful sentence:

> 2C. Neither Mrs. Smith nor her attorney has contacted the bank.

3. Let the verb do the work in a sentence; let the verb carry the weight of the sentence. (Unless you are a skillful writer, beware of sentence fragments without a verb.) Concentrate in your writing or speaking on finding the strongest, most effective, and most powerful verb to give the particular meaning you wish to convey. Conversely, if you do not wish to convey your meaning clearly or directly, use a weak verb or use a passive.

This example shows a stuffy, trite opening to a letter, using a weak verb:

3A. We are in receipt of your letter of December 9.

The key word in this sentence is "receipt." Turn this into a verb and the sentence reads:

3B. We have received your letter of December 9.

Now go one step further (this belongs under the final guide Be human) and use a standard courteous opening:

3C. Thank you for your letter of December 9.

4. This sentence uses the passive voice, too many words, and does not state the actor:

4A. During the month of January, this product was in the process of being evaluated.

This sentence can be pruned, but the passive cannot be changed to active until we know who is doing the evaluating. If we assume that it was the writer's organization, then the sentence reads as follows:

4B. During January, we evaluated this product.

If, on the other hand, someone else was doing the evaluating, then sentence 4A is ambiguous.

5. Always use active verbs in instruction writing. For example:

5A. This machine should be given a careful inspection before each use.

Changing the verb to the imperative form solves the problem here:

5B. Inspect the machine carefully before each use.

Note the unsatisfactory weak passive verb "should be given" in 5A. Does "should" mean "must" or "may"? Is the inspection mandatory, or is it optional? Also, who does the inspecting? The use of the passive here without the name of the actor creates an ambiguity which might be important to resolve.

6. Sometimes passive verbs and the failure to name the actor arise because of a policy within the organization that discourages the writer from identifying himself. This sentence, for example, appeared in a letter to a client written by an accountant in a firm which had a strong policy requiring that everything should be done in the name of the firm:

> 6A. In continuation of our telephone conversation regarding valuation of securities owned through separate accounts, it is suggested that a written consistent policy be adopted.

Who did the suggesting? Apparently the writer meant the following:

> 6B. Confirming our phone conversation regarding valuation of securities owned through separate accounts, I (we?) suggest that you adopt a written consistent policy.

7. Here is another example of the indefinite "it," this time referring to the reader rather than the writer:

> 7A. If it is felt that the adoption of this procedure is unacceptable because it would require employing two additional personnel, we suggest . . .

Again, we can only guess at the writer's meaning, but probably it is this:

> 7B. If you believe that adopting this procedure is unacceptable because it would require you to employ two additional people, we suggest . . .

Note also the change from "personnel" to "people" in 7B. The impersonal word "personnel" allows us to think of human beings as a mass of numbers in a computer, to be manipulated at will. The word "people," on the other hand, helps remind us that the other employees in our organization are individual, distinct human beings just like ourselves, with individual, distinct people problems.

BE CLEAR

How will they understand your words?

Are you using words that are clear to your audience and not just clear to yourself and your associates? This guide requires you to go back to the three People Questions in Step 1 and to consider your audience. Who are they? What is their environment? What do you know about them? How much knowledge do they have of the subject you are communicating to them, and therefore what words and phrases can you safely use without explaining their meaning carefully?

Like Be direct, this guide helps remind you of the problems created by poor word order, discussed under Step 4. These problems lead us to a failure to be clear, not because the wrong word was used but because words were placed in the wrong part of the sentence.

1. In-house jargon is a common cause for a failure to be clear. The jargon is not necessarily gobbledygook in the sense that it is made up of pompous polysyllables, but nonetheless the words have acquired a special meaning that the reader or listener will not understand.

For example, the mayor of a town that was building a reservoir wrote to a government agency to inquire as to prevailing practices in other communities concerning the use of reservoirs for recreational purposes. The letter the mayor received stated that in certain communities reservoirs are open to such limited recreation uses as fishing, boating, picnicking and camping, but, the letter continued:

Body contact activities are strictly prohibited.

The reader of this sentence could well be pardoned for believing that this prohibition referred to some new type of esoteric sexual activity. However, its meaning was far more innocent. For the purposes of this prohibition "body contact activities" meant, believe it or not, swimming; when you swim, your body is in contact with the water of the reservoir!

2. Punctuation, or lack of it, can sometimes cause confusion. A specification for military uniforms contained this phrase:

Materials shall consist of blue, green and grey fibers.

The specifications were for three different colors of fibers: blue, green, and grey. One manufacturer read the specification as requiring two kinds of uniforms: one that was blue and the other containing a mixture of green and grey fibers. The resulting confusion wasted everyone's time.

The misplaced comma can frequently be a real cause of trouble, when a comma is either inserted where it should not be or omitted, as in this case, where it should be. Thus, if the phrase had read, "Materials shall consist of blue, green, and grey fibers," there would have been no possibility of misunderstanding.

3. In the next example, the combining of gobbledygook with uncertain word order and meaning results in a failure to be clear.

The building superintendent of a large office building in the suburbs was inspecting the outside of the building with the vice-president in charge of building operations when the vice-president pointed out to him that weeds were growing rather vigorously in some of the shrubbery beds. The superintendent, chagrined to have the vice-president point this out to him, and anxious to follow proper corporate style, promptly sent a memo to his foreman telling him to:

Eliminate the undesirable vegetation around the perimeter of the building.

From long experience, the foreman knew that his boss, the superintendent, was a Theory X type who expected the foreman to do as he was told. The foreman, however, read the message as saying that all the vegetation around the building was undesirable. His job was not to reason why but to carry out orders, so he quickly instructed his men to remove all the vegetation, including the newly planted shrubs.

Is this an absurd result? Not when you combine a Theory X manager, gobbledygook, writing to impress rather than to express, and a failure to be clear. How much simpler if the superintendent had simply said "Joe, get rid of those weeds."

Beware of Unnecessary Memos

The written message is frequently a less satisfactory means of communication than the spoken message. In the previous example, it seems hardly possible that if the superintendent were speaking to Joe, he would have told him to "eliminate the undesirable vegetation." If he had, Joe would have undoubtedly asked, "What do you mean?" By choosing to write, the superintendent was deprived of Joe's feedback.

When you write, you do not know whether your audience will read your message; and, if they do read it, whether they will understand it the way you intended and therefore whether you will get the action you want and thus achieve your purpose. But when you talk to someone on the phone or face-to-face, if he does not understand your message, the probability is greater (but by no means certain) that he will ask you to explain.

A simple, short memo costs at least $4, if you count the writer's and typist's time. A three-minute phone call anywhere in the country costs less than half that amount; even if you follow up the phone call with a confirming memo, you are better off, because during the phone call you had the benefit of a two-way discussion.

In most large organizations, greater use of the phone and of face-to-face contact would save many hours spent in writing unnecessary memos. If a record is needed, and it often is, then after the conversation, the person desiring the record can write a memo for the file and send a copy to the other interested parties; but this kind of confirming memo is far less work to write than the initial memo stating the question, problem, or instruction.

To the outsider looking in, the absurdities to which memo writing is carried within large organizations are sometimes hard to believe, except perhaps in instances where the memo writers do not have enough work to do and therefore are illustrating Parkinson's law: "Work expands so as to fill the time available for its completion."[17]

For example, in a large insurance company there was a division responsible for preparing complex special risk policies. When a question arose about the appropriate language to use in a new policy, the assistant manager in the division would send a carefully written three- to four-page memo to a lawyer in the legal division.

The lawyer would study the memo carefully, spend several hours researching the question, possibly but rarely discuss it with the assistant manager, and then prepare an equally detailed precise three- or four-page answer. The lawyer would first write the answer out almost completely in longhand and then would dictate it to his secretary from his voluminous notes.

Because of the thoroughness with which he researched the questions and the length of his memos (copies of which were circulated to the general counsel), the lawyer writing the memos was in due course promoted. The assistant manager from time to time found that the lawyer's memos answering his questions were not always responsive to the question, were not always exactly what he wanted, or, by the time the memos had been exchanged, were no longer needed; but, at

[17] C. Northcote Parkinson, *Parkinson's Law*. Boston: Houghton Mifflin Company, 1957.

any rate, he had a solid, substantial file of legal memos and could never be criticized for failure to consult the legal division on questionaole policy provisions.

After awhile, the assistant manager found he was spending several hours a week writing these memos. This helped him in requesting another assistant to relieve him of some of the burden of his increasing workload; likewise, because of the time the lawyer required to prepare his answers, he in turn felt he could justify recommending an increase in legal division personnel.

The assistant manager's boss was a skillful empire builder and therefore was heartedly in favor of anything that created more work for his division. The general counsel of the legal division was equally concerned with building up the prestige of his division and therefore encouraged his lawyers to write detailed memos.

But apparently what everyone overlooked, perhaps because they wanted to overlook it, was that this memo-writing process was about 80 percent unnecessary. If the assistant manager had come to the lawyer's desk in each case with the facts of the particular case in hand, and if they had discussed it orally for perhaps half an hour, there would have been no necessity to write a memo in most of the cases, except perhaps a short confirming one for the files.

BE HUMAN

People communicate with people.

Never forget that your audience is made up of living, breathing, individual human beings like yourself, who, like yourself, have individual, personal fears, needs, problems, hopes, and goals.

When you talk face-to-face with other people, you are less likely to forget this (although sometimes the Theory X manager does forget), but how easy it is, in writing a memo or a letter, for you, me, or anyone else to forget that the audience for our message consists of people like ourselves. Be human, therefore, brings us squarely back to the three People Questions in Step 1 and to the use of the motivators in Step 2.

Many of the examples that illustrate a failure to be human come from letters to customers or to the public, written by supervisors and lower-level managers who feel their primary responsibility is to process a minimum number of transactions each day. Understandably, to such people the customer is simply a number that identifies the transaction.

These typical examples of this attitude are from letters to customers:

1. Your failure to complete item 9 on the application form, which is returned herewith, makes it impossible for us to do other than withhold your certificate.
2. Since you overlooked giving us your client's address, we are not in a position to furnish him with the information he needs.
3. We have to advise that you may defer this action.
4. You misunderstood the statement in our letter of April 16.

Better substitutes for each of above which would certainly antagonize the customer less would be as follows:

1. Item 9 on the application form is not completed. If you will complete this and return the form to us, we will issue your certificate.
2. You did not tell us your client's address. If you will send us this, we will furnish him with the information he needs.
3. You may defer this action.
4. Your understanding of the statement in our letter of April 16 was apparently different from ours.

This letter was written by an assistant secretary of a small bank to a customer who had complained of long teller lines:

Dear Mr. Reinhold:

We acknowledge receipt of your letter of March 12.

Hitherto no customer has ever complained about slow service. It has been our policy to man our tellers' cages for the maximum peak of activity. We regret that you had to wait and shall try to determine the cause.

It surprises me that the attitude of one of our employees displeased you. We had instructed all personnel to be courteous. We shall speak to them again about this matter.

Very truly yours,

If this utterly tactless letter was characteristic of letters this bank wrote to their customers or of the way the customers were treated by tellers, no wonder the bank remained small. This letter bristles with hostility toward the customer; clearly, to the writer (who was in charge of the tellers), customers were a nuisance to be tolerated. He felt that his job was to oversee the processing of transactions. Customers were simply incidental to those transactions.

Such an attitude is unfortunately prevalent in any administrative unit of any organization that must handle many inquiries, questions, complaints, or transactions from customers, unless those in charge of the unit make a serious and continuing effort to remind their employees that customers are people, not numbers in a computer. Because administrative employees often have little contact with the customer, this reminder is needed regularly.

Another example of a failure to be human is seen in Case 2—No Job for Alice Green. This case applied the People Questions to a cold, tactless letter written by an employment interviewer who, in her job, certainly should have known better. The letter read:

Dear Miss Green:

We have completed our review of your application and test

results. We find we are unable to offer a position to you at this time.

> Very truly yours,
>
> M. C. Rush
> Personnel Department

The revision of this letter suggested in Case 2 read as follows:

Dear Alice:

Thank you for applying for a job at our bank.

We have carefully reviewed your application. I am sorry to tell you we cannot offer you a position now.

> Sincerely,
> Mary C. Rush,
> Employment Interviewer

A comparison of the two letters emphasizes the curt language of the first. The opening lacks ordinary business courtesy; the use of "we find" immediately after "test results" strongly implies Miss Green was too stupid to hire; no effort is made to explain why she failed to qualify; and the salutation "Very truly yours" is cold by today's standards.

Impersonal, tactless, unclear language frequently appears in forms and form letters designed by lower-level administrators to handle repetitive situations. The usual pattern is that a letter is individually written to handle a particular situation; the next time a similar situation occurs, the carbon of the first letter is marked up slightly, and the same wording is used again. Gradually, the first letter becomes a form letter, to be used in every situation that more or less resembles the original one, but at no point along the line does anyone stand back and examine the wording critically to see if it is appropriate, courteous, and customer-oriented.

The guide—Be human—also serves as an important reminder, at the choice-of-words level, of Theory X and Theory Y. Tactful, considerate, courteous words are far more likely to appeal to anyone's ego needs than the curt words of the examples shown above, whether these words are written or oral.

To solve the problem presented by a failure to be human, we need to do more than merely criticize the words—we need to look behind the words to the behavior of the writer or speaker. It does little good to tell him his words are tactless, unless we can also somehow change his behavior.

When you write or speak, what do the words you use reveal about your behavior toward people?

Step 6
Write Effectively

This step is concerned with the act of writing itself. This is the point at which you begin to put words on paper, applying the principles of the Behind the Words system as you do so. This step has three guides:

- Dictate a rough draft from an outline.
- Scan your draft first.
- Edit your draft vigorously.

DICTATE A ROUGH DRAFT FROM AN OUTLINE

To write your message efficiently, and to produce the best quality, dictate to a machine a rough draft from your poker chip outline. If you have a substantial amount of writing in the course of a business week, this is also the cheapest method for your organization.

The lingering opposition to the use of dictating machines found in some organizations and among some managers, professionals, and their secretaries is primarily a resistance to change and a failure to understand, or perhaps a failure to want to understand, the advantages of dictating. Coupled with this may be a fear of the equipment or a fear that the dictator somehow exposes himself to ridicule by talking his thoughts onto the machine in something less than flawless sentences.

Note the requirements for successful dictating—(1) to a machine, (2) a rough draft, (3) from your poker chip outline. Let's look at these in order.

Dictate to a Machine

First, why is it more efficient to dictate to a machine as opposed to any other method of getting the writing job done? Dictating to a machine is, on the average, four times as fast as longhand. You or I can talk at speeds up to 120 words a minute, but we cannot write in longhand at more than 30 words a minute. This time-saving alone is enough to justify the use of dictating machines for heavy writers.

But more important is the improvement in quality. When you are dictating to a machine, you are working much closer to the speed of your mind and you are not bogged down by the tedious drudgery of longhand. More effectively than any other method, dictating encourages you to use the creative side of your mind.

As you talk your ideas on to the machine, the creative part of your mind is at work generating new ideas. Sometimes these new ideas relate to the immediate subject, such as a better way of phrasing the sentence you are dictating. Before you forget the idea, you can dictate it.

Sometimes the new ideas relate to something you said earlier or plan to say later. In those cases, dictate this creative idea before you forget it, with a note to yourself to move it to somewhere in the finished product. Don't rely on your memory; by the time you get to the right place, you will have forgotten the idea.

Dictating also prevents you from editing before you have finished getting your words on paper. The analytical process of editing cannot, for most people, be successfully combined with the creative process of writing. Yet the longhand writer, unless he has carefully trained himself, inevitably finds himself editing his sentences as he writes them and thus losing the creative flow of ideas.

Is this creativity important to the manager handling his daily correspondence or is it important only to the novelist? The term "creative writing" is often used to describe the writing of fiction; does this mean that there is no real creativity in other forms of writing? The answer to these questions is that there is room for creativity in anything we do, at home or at work, that does not follow an established, set pattern. The manager, for example, who finds a better way of answering the customer's inquiry is using his creative ability, although he may be using a different kind of creativity than the novelist.

Why the emphasis in this guide on dictating to a machine instead of to a secretary? First, secretaries are expensive and increasingly scarce; junior and middle managers sometimes have difficulty in obtaining their own secretary. Second, if you have your own secretary, dictating to her through a machine saves time and money for everyone. She need not be sitting at your side while you think and dictate; if the phone rings, you need not wonder whether to let her go or to keep her waiting while you talk. If you dictate to her through a machine, she is free to do something else the entire time that you are dictating. The cost of the machine is paid for by her greater efficiency. Third, unless your secretary is experienced, you can dictate faster to a machine, thus saving your own time.

The cost figures that follow, intentionally stated conservatively, show how quickly dictating equipment pays for itself.

Assume a manager's salary is $15,000 per year, or $7.50 per hour. His secretary receives $125 per week, or $3.12 per hour. He dictates for one-half hour per day and, because he normally dictates a rough draft, he requires ten minutes to edit the draft. Assume that the typing time equals the dictating time (probably the typist types a little slower than the dictator talks, but on the other hand, the dictator frequently pauses for thought, so the assumption that typing time equals dictating time seems a reasonable one).

The cost per day for one-half hour of dictation, ten minutes of editing, plus typing and retyping, is as follows:

DICTATOR'S TIME	COST	SECRETARY'S TIME	COST
½ hour	$3.75	½ hour	$1.56
10 min.	1.25	½ hour	1.56
	$5.00		$3.12

Total $8.12

Now assume that the manager writes out his message in longhand. Since writing in longhand is four times slower than dictating to a machine, his time will now cost $3.75 × 4, or $15. The typing time remains the same, $1.56, and, to keep the figures conservative, assume that no second typing is required. (The first longhand draft is in final form.) The total costs are now $16.56, or almost exactly twice the cost of dictating.

On the basis of this simple example, with conservative estimates and only one-half hour of dictating per day, longhand is twice as expensive as dictating. If the manager were to continue to write one-half hour per day for one year, or 240 working days, the savings through using dictating equipment would be $1,920.

A complete individual dictating system, including a desk dictating machine for the manager, a desk transcriber for the secretary, and a pocket-sized portable for the manager to take home at night or on a trip, costs about one-half (depending on the manufacturer) of the one-year's saving. Under these assumptions, dictating equipment will have paid for itself in six months.

These figures are conservative. If the manager's salary is $30,000 or if he dictates one hour per day, dictating equipment will pay for itself sooner. If several dictators share the same machine or use a telephone dictating system with a transcriber located on a nearby secretary's desk, then equipment costs are less. Also, our example assumes that the dictator will always dictate a rough draft but will always write the finished product in longhand the first time. Many managers prefer a rough draft, even when writing their message entirely in longhand.

At this point, an important warning should be noted. Systems analysts and accountants working with figures such as the above often conclude that the cheapest and most efficient option would be a telephone dictating system with the transcribing being done by typists working in a central pool, usually remote from the dictator and mutually unknown to each other.

On paper, this looks fine, but it ignores some vital human factors. As a result, many organizations have found that their elaborately installed and expensive central dictating system is not working the way they had hoped it would.

Why? What usually happens is that managers and professionals in the organization use the system a few times, but find that service is too slow or, more important, that the anonymous typist in the central pool does not do a satisfactory job on the more complex letters and reports. She does not know the language of the dictator, she does not know his voice, and perhaps most important, she does not know him as a person. To her, the message she is transcribing is just one more item to be done in a day's work. The process is totally impersonal. If the dictator finds his copy is full of errors, he cannot conveniently go back to the typist who made the errors and explain to her in person what his requirements are. So, after a few unsatisfactory experiences like this, the dictator gives up and goes back to longhand.

Central dictating with an impersonal typing pool is satisfactory for simple routine correspondence where the dictator is so familiar with the material that he can dictate a final draft the first time, and where the typist can become familiar with the pattern of the correspondence. Even here, finding girls to work in a central typing pool is not easy, because the job is so mechanical.

All modern dictating equipment uses an erasable magnetic tape, or belt. This has eliminated a valid objection that applied to older machines. When the dictator makes an error, he simply rewinds, listens to what he has said, then rewinds again to the point at which the error occurred and redictates, automatically erasing with his new words what he has previously said. Earlier dictating machines did not have magnetic tape, or belts, and therefore older managers may remember the unsatisfactory experience of dictating corrections and explaining to the typist where the correction was to be inserted. This clumsy process has been eliminated by the magnetic equipment.

Secretaries sometimes resist the introduction of dictating machines because they feel that they will lose direct contact with their boss. This need not be so. On the contrary, they should find that their job is more interesting, that they have more time to spend on more important things, and that their day-to-day contact with their boss is in no way hurt by the dictating equipment.

This discussion has advocated dictating as opposed to longhand for the rough draft. If you are a reasonably good typist, don't overlook the advantages of typing your drafts (not the final copy). Many professional writers consistently type their drafts. Typing is probably twice as fast as longhand under these circumstances; it has the advantage of allowing you to see what you have written, yet prevents you from wholesale editing until you have finished getting your ideas on paper.

In some offices, a foolish idea persists that typewriters are only for clerks; managers are not allowed to have typewriters. Such an idea ignores the time-saving advantages of the typewriter for those whose writing duties are heavy.

Dictate a Rough Draft

The second point in this guide is to dictate a rough draft. Don't attempt, unless you are very familiar with the subject matter, to dictate the finished copy the first time. Almost no one can do that. Frequently, a new dictator will feel that he must dictate flawless copies the first time no matter how complex or new his material may be. After a few unsuccessful attempts to do this, he becomes discouraged and stops dictating.

Don't expect to dictate anything other than a rough draft, particularly of complex or new material. In the dictating process, you are getting your ideas down on paper without the laborious drudgery of longhand. Let the words flow freely. Don't be too concerned if your sentences are sloppy or long-winded. Your mind is working creatively, and the process of dictating in itself generates more ideas. Get these ideas down while they are fresh in your mind. Do not attempt to carefully edit your sentences as you dictate; if you do, you interfere with the creative process.

On the other hand, if you are dictating letters or reports that are short and simple, or that follow a familiar pattern which you have dictated many times before, you can expect to dictate these in final form the first time, particularly if you have a copy of the previous letter or report in front of you.

Don't be concerned that the secretary or typist transcribing your work will feel you are stupid because your rough-draft sentences are somewhat less than flawless. Simply tell her at the beginning that this is a rough draft which you want double-spaced. This saves her time because she does not need to make a carbon and she does not need to be so careful in correcting errors. At the same time, this tells her that you will not be dictating flawless sentences. Remember also that typists cannot type and think about the substance of what they are typing at the same time. The typist therefore cannot analyze the merits of your sentences as she types them.

Dictate from Your Poker Chip Outline

The third point in this guide is to dictate from your poker chip outline. Again, this assumes you are dictating a lengthy, complex message on a relatively new subject. Obviously, if you are writing a letter of three short paragraphs on a familiar subject, you don't need to dictate it from an elaborate outline (although you should review in your mind for at least a moment what you plan to say, before you start to talk).

When you start to dictate a complex message, have in front of you a poker chip outline that at least shows the blue chips and red chips in your message; if the message is longer, you will need greater detail than that. Follow this outline as you dictate, but don't be surprised if you find that the outline requires change. The dictating process generates new and better ideas. If your outline is too detailed, you will find either that you have restricted yourself to too tight a framework or else that you must change substantially the outline you have so carefully prepared. Remember that your poker chip outline is not an elaborate outline of the type taught in college with Roman numerals, capital letters, etc. This is your own personal, informal working outline.

Sometimes, if your message is to be reviewed by others, you will save everyone's time by tidying up your outline a little and presenting it first to the various reviewers for their approval. This shows them the general direction in which you plan to go, so that any differences of opinion can be discussed at a concept level without becoming bogged down in the minutiae of words. Some reviewers do not understand the advantages of this technique, but it can be a most useful one.

Outlining is hard work requiring orderly, organized thinking. We all tend to shortcut or slight this process, feeling that we can save time by getting right to the words themselves; but the good writer knows that in the long run he does not save time when he attempts to write without an adequate outline. The extensive revision necessary ultimately uses as much or more time as if he had started with a good outline.

SCAN YOUR DRAFT FIRST

When your typed draft is ready for your editing, do not pick up your editorial pencil and start by correcting the first words in the first sentence. Put your pencil down; sit back and scan the draft first. ("Scan" means both a close examination of something and a quick inspection of something. In this book, it is used only in the latter sense.)

As you scan your draft, review the People Questions. Is your purpose clear? Have you fully considered all your audience and what they want from this message? Have you used motivators effectively whenever you could? Is your poker chip outline a sound one? Will it be clear to your audience? Do you see sentences and paragraphs that are too wordy or too long? Is there repetition of ideas? Are certain ideas out of place; should they be moved to somewhere else?

Ask yourself these questions as you scan. When you find something that needs editing or correction, mark it in the margin with perhaps a word or two to remind yourself of the problem; but don't stop to correct it now. You are scanning the entire message for overall content and overall substance. If you stop to correct and edit, you will lose the all important continuity of thought and you may find that you are editing unnecessarily, since the correction you inserted might be affected by something you wrote later on.

If you possibly can, set aside for the scanning process a time when you will not be interrupted. Interruptions destroy the continuity of thought that you seek while scanning.

Reviewing Your Subordinate's Writing

If you are reviewing a subordinate's writing, scan it also before you pick up your editorial pencil. Try to leave the detailed editing to the writer. When you do this, you are properly delegating editorial responsibility. Your job as a reviewer should be primarily to satisfy yourself that the content and substance of the message are correct. Thus, it should be more of a scanning than a detailed editing.

If you insist, as some reviewers do, on changes that reflect your own personal style, you destroy your subordinate's initiative. At this point, he may well say to himself, "If you're going to make that many changes, why not write it yourself?" If you have delegated to the subordinate the task of writing a particular letter or report, then recognize that he can never write it exactly the way you would. Above all, do not make changes simply to show him that you are the boss. (Some reviewers do just this, particularly in those cases where there are several levels of review and the reviewer in the middle feels that he must make changes to show to his boss he has spent sufficient time in the review process.)

When you do make changes in your subordinate's writing, explain to him why you made the changes. He deserves this explanation from you. If you cannot explain the changes, except on grounds of personal taste, then ask yourself whether the changes are really necessary.

If you identify problem areas in your review, but then allow the subordinate to make the changes himself, you are delegating editorial responsibility and saving yourself a great deal of time. Also, you are training your subordinate so he will write better in the future. Finally, you are avoiding the common error of changing a phrase in one place without realizing the same phrase occurs elsewhere and thus should be changed throughout. A reviewer who does too much editing himself can easily make this error; he does not know the overall content of the message as well as the writer does.

Failure to delegate editorial responsibility causes particular problems in letters written by middle-management people in federal agencies. In some agencies, routine letters are reviewed by as many as four reviewers, some of them at much too high a level.

The following example illustrates the absurdities of this overreview process. The letter, written by a middle-management specialist in answer to a routine inquiry, was reviewed at four levels (the process took six weeks) before mailing. As originally written, the letter read as follows:

Dear Mr. Smith:

In further reply to your letter of May 14, I am enclosing a table which shows the number of persons living in Florida who were receiving benefits as of December 1969. Totals are presented for the entire state and for each county.

Similar information is not available directly for Miami Beach. However, we do have data for the area encompassed by postal zip code 33139. A total of 25,000 persons receiving mail through that zip code were on the benefit roles at the end of 1969. You should be aware that the postal delivery area encompassed by postal zip code 33139 may differ from the actual physical boundaries of Miami Beach. There could thus be a possible discrepancy in the data.

I hope this information will be of help to you.

Sincerely yours,

The first reviewer changed "December 1969" to "December

31, 1969" and made no other changes. The second reviewer (one level higher than the first reviewer) made no changes. Obviously, both believed in delegating editorial responsibility.

The third reviewer (one level higher still) added the clause "which includes Miami Beach" at the end of the second sentence in the second paragraph and changed "actual physical" to "political." The first change perhaps clears up an ambiguity. The second change is nitpicking.

The fourth reviewer, the most senior man, was even more nitpicking in his changes. Apparently he had a personal prejudice against beginning a sentence with the word "however," so he felt it necessary to combine the first two sentences in the second paragraph, omit the "however," and start the sentence with "although." In the next sentence, he changed "receiving mail through" to "within." In the last sentence of the paragraph, he changed "there could thus be a possible discrepancy in the data" to read "you should be aware that this could result in a possible discrepancy in the data." After these earthshaking changes were made, the letter was retyped and sent for signature to the bureau chief, one level higher still. The final letter read as follows:

Dear Mr. Smith:

In further reply to your letter of May 14, I am enclosing a table which shows the number of persons living in Florida who were receiving benefits as of December 31, 1969. Totals are presented for the entire state and for each county.

Although similar information is not available directly for Miami Beach, we do have data for the area encompassed by postal zip code 33139 which includes Miami Beach. A total of 25,000 persons within that zip code were on the benefit roles at the end of 1969.

You should be aware that the postal delivery area encompassed by postal zip code 33139 may differ from the political boundaries of Miami Beach. You should be aware that this could result in a possible discrepancy in the data.

I hope this information will be of help to you.

Sincerely yours,

Such a process of thorough overreview on a routine letter is enormously wasteful of everyone's time and destructive to a subordinate's initiative. One wonders why this routine letter could not have been signed by the subordinate who wrote it, with no review. Probably the answer is fear—fear that the agency will be criticized by a hostile congressman or unfriendly reporter unless every piece of writing is exhaustively overreviewed and signed at too high a level.

EDIT YOUR DRAFT VIGOROUSLY

This is the last step in the writing process. You have scanned your draft and marked problem areas, words, or sentences. Now pick up your editorial pencil, and, applying all the principles discussed so far in the Behind the Words system, edit your draft as vigorously and as thoroughly as your time will permit and the circumstances require.

If the message is important to you personally or to your organization, take enough time to do a thorough, intelligent, and critical editorial job. If the message is vitally important, don't be afraid to go through two or three more drafts; each time you will have a better product. Keep at it until you are satisfied.

On the other hand, don't waste time on an elaborate, detailed, careful review if the message really isn't worth that much time. To decide how much time to spend, review the People Questions. What is your purpose? How important is it to you that the message be as perfect as you can make it? In some cases, this is important, and in some cases, it really isn't. It is always important that your message be clear to your audience, but it may not always be important to strive for perfection in style.

How do you edit vigorously? This skill is developed only by practice. You must learn to stand outside and look at your own writing critically, as if you were a third person. The inexperienced writer finds this very difficult at first. If you have trouble being sufficiently critical and objective with your own writing, put it aside at least overnight and then look at it fresh and after your mind has been occupied on something else. You may be surprised to find that sentences which seemed so flawless when you wrote them now seem full of flaws.

As you edit, be ruthless in pruning out the unnecessary words and clauses. Be savage in cutting down the gobbledy-gook and substituting simple, clear, everyday words. Be harsh with yourself as you examine your pet words and phrases. Are they really as effective as you think? If you're not sure, cut them out.

It often helps in the longer message to have a working table of contents handy as you edit. This allows you to check back and see where the particular paragraph you are reading fits into the overall structure.

Edit with a pencil and an eraser, not a pen, so that you can change your mind.

Whenever possible, ask someone else to read your draft. He will look at it from a fresh point of view and will see problems you overlooked.

Remember that editing is a different process from writing. When you dictated your rough draft, you were to a large extent using the creative side of your mind, within the framework of your poker chip outline. The editing process is more analytical. You are examining the product of your creative mind critically to see how good a job you did and to change what needs to be changed.

The editorial process is more easily interrupted than the

creative process of getting the words down on paper. You can have a draft on your desk and edit it between interruptions without the serious loss of continuity that would occur if you had attempted to write the original message this way.

Skillful writers are above all skillful editors. No matter how brilliant your ideas may be, your communication expressing those ideas will not be brilliant unless you subject it to vigorous editing.

Read Effectively

This step requires only a few pages because most of the principles for effective reading have already been covered in the earlier steps in this book. This step, which collects and refers back to these principles, has three guides:

- Preread the message first.
- Choose your reading speed.
- Read for the poker chip structure.

The guides to effective reading covered in this step do not pretend to accomplish all that a full program of speed reading would accomplish, but rather are limited to some simple principles which will help you read more effectively on the job. Speed reading is a specialized skill which takes time to learn and, once learned, is easily forgotten unless practiced regularly. If you are a student, or if you have a special need to scan masses of written information daily, then a speed reading course would be valuable and the necessary reading in your daily work would mean that you could maintain your speed.

PREREAD THE MESSAGE FIRST

What process do you follow as you take each item from the in-box on your desk? Do you read each item carefully from start to finish, putting aside everything else until you have done so? Or have you developed a technique for prereading the item first? Most of us who have any volume of incoming mail, whether internal or external, have been forced to develop a prereading technique.

For example, suppose your subordinate has returned from an inspection trip to three of your company's plants. His job was to determine whether the personnel people in each plant were following the latest changes in the regulations prohibiting discrimination in hiring practices. His report is in your in-box.

How do you preread it? The steps you take, and they would require less time than it takes you to read them here, could be as follows:

1. You glance quickly at the "to," "from," and "subject" lines of the report. This tells you that it is addressed to you, sent by your subordinate, and concerns his inspection trip. This first glance also gives you a partial answer to the three People Questions. His purpose is to tell you about the trip. He is involved along with personnel people in three plants and personnel people concerned with employment practices in the head office where you are; you don't know yet who else is involved. You may not yet be sure what you want, other than a report you can read quickly and understand without difficulty.

2. Next, you note the number of pages, because this will suggest how much time you will need to read it and therefore whether you should read it in its entirety now or simply scan it and put it aside for detailed reading later.

3. Now you look for a summary of his findings and recommendations. If your subordinate has followed a point-first

approach, you should find this on the first page. At this point, you read the summary carefully. If you don't find a summary on the first page, you may start hunting for it or at least looking for some clues as to the structure of the report.

4. After you find the summary and read it carefully, the prereading process is over. Now you are ready to make a decision that will lead you to the next step in effective reading, namely, choosing your reading speed.

5. But, on the other hand, if you do not find a quick and convenient summary, then you continue your prereading process by scanning the message to find out what it is all about and thus in effect developing your own summary. This will be a high-speed turning of pages, reading of opening and closing sentences to sections or paragraphs, and looking for key thoughts that will give you a feeling for the content of the message as a whole. If the report is poorly structured, you will have to waste your time doing this.

The prereading process has been described here for a report from a subordinate. With such a report, the prereading might take no more than a few seconds. The process is similar, although it may require more time, with anything else you take from your in-box. The less familiar you are with the writer or the subject matter, the more time you may need for the prereading.

CHOOSE YOUR READING SPEED

Having preread the message, your next decision is to choose your reading speed. Continuing with the example of the hiring practices report from your subordinate, suppose that the prereading leads you to a first-page summary which tells you that all three plants are doing what they should be doing and that no serious problems are apparent.

This reassuring statement would suggest to you that you need not read the balance of the report carefully, although probably you still want to scan it. Therefore you choose a fast reading speed. This means that you push yourself to scan the report critically but quickly, to see if there is anything of importance not covered by the summary and to perhaps see if the writer's conclusions seem warranted by the facts he presents.

Your scanning of his comments on the first plant leads you to perceive no problems, so you move on to his comments on the second plant. As you read this, you become concerned. Something seems wrong. You wonder if he talked to the right people in the second plant. Now your reading speed slows down. You go back a few paragraphs and read again what he said about the second plant. Then perhaps you compare the two, reading slowly and critically, either until you are satisfied or until you decide that you will have to discuss this with him further in person. And so it goes, with the reading speed not only varying from message to message, but frequently varying within a message.

Much of the process described here is one that many of us follow instinctively everyday, adjusting our reading speeds to suit the material we are reading.

But some managers have never learned this valuable technique, or if they have learned it, are afraid to use it. They feel the only safe course is to read everything at the same plodding speed, starting at word 1 of sentence 1 and going through to the end.

If you are such a manager, if you have never used the time-saving advantages of prereading and choosing your reading speed, don't be afraid to try it. At first you may do better to try it at home on a newspaper, a magazine, or a book. As you read the morning paper, push yourself. Scan the first page to identify the stories you want to read. Look at the headlines; then read the first two or three sentences of the story.

Reporters traditionally follow the inverted-pyramid formula in their stories, requiring that they state the who, what, when, where, why, and how at the very beginning of the story (another application of point first). Don't read beyond this point-first opening unless the story interests you, but do read the point-first opening carefully enough so that you know what the story is all about. Unfortunately, the traditional newspaper lead sometimes compresses so much into the opening sentence that your reading time must slow down to understand it.

Suppose you decide to read further, but only for general information. Start reading, but consciously push yourself to read as fast as you can without losing the meaning of the story. Try to avoid regressing, i.e., going back and rereading words you have already read. This common habit is a real time-waster, and worse still, destroys continuity of thought. Read for thoughts, not individual words.

If this process seems difficult or unfamiliar to you, read more at home (and watch television less). The more you read at home, the easier your reading becomes at the office, particularly if you practice at home the techniques of prereading and of selectively choosing different reading speeds.

READ FOR THE POKER CHIP STRUCTURE

As you read, look for the poker chip structure of the message. What are the writer's blue chips? What are his red chips? What is the overall structure of his message? If this is a well-structured business message, you will have little difficulty in answering these questions, but if it is not, you may have real difficulty.

As you look for the poker chip structure, ask yourself the People Questions:

■   What is your purpose as reader? If you can answer this question as soon as you start to read, your reading will be much easier because you will know what to look for as you read.

- Who is the writer? What do you know about him? What is his environment? What is his relationship to you? Who else will read this? What do you know about them?
- What does the writer want? What action or result does he seek from you or others?

If you are reading a letter or report whose poker chip structure is not clear, take out your pencil and underline key words or phrases to help you find your way back through the material when you read it a second time. Underline key phrases only — heavy underlining becomes confusing and destroys readability.

Don't read every word carefully in the message. Don't take the time to analyze or study a particular choice of words unless it is important to you to understand or question it.

A final word on effective reading. Always read critically. Too many of us have a reverence for the printed or typed word that is unjustified. Because we see it in print, we feel it must be so, forgetting that every writer is a person like ourselves — fallible, human, emotional. Perhaps he is careful and thorough, perhaps not. Perhaps he took time to say exactly what he meant, perhaps not. Perhaps he was in a hurry. Perhaps he is skillfully and consciously using words which will express his prejudices in a subtle and clever way that he hopes we as readers will not recognize. Perhaps he is doing the same thing unconsciously. In any case, remember that just because the words are in print, they are not necessarily endowed with some greater authority than they would have if spoken.

Step 8
Listen and Speak Effectively

This final step in the Behind the Words system collects the principles for effective listening and speaking.

This step is primarily concerned with face-to-face communications, which can be defined as conversations with a purpose. Most managers spend most of their day listening and speaking to subordinates, superiors, associates, and customers. Yet few of us have had adequate training in the complex skills required for effective listening and speaking face to face.

Listening and speaking are included together in this step because they are not separate processes in face-to-face communications. While you are speaking, you are (or should be) watching for signs from your audience to show how effectively you are getting across. While you are listening, you are often planning your next statement (sometimes to the exclusion of effective listening).

In the formal oral presentation, as distinguished from

face-to-face communications, the skills of effective listening and speaking are to a greater extent separate processes. While you are speaking, I am listening. The feedback you perceive from my reactions to your words may lead you to change your presentation as you go along, but usually these changes will be slight unless I interrupt you to express a positive reaction. The more formal the presentation, the less likely are such interruptions.

In considering the processes of listening and speaking, it is often convenient to divide oral business communications into two broad categories—the first, reporting, and the second, interviewing.

When you are reporting to or instructing one or more people in your organization, whether they are superiors, associates, or subordinates, your purpose is to furnish them with certain information and, probably, to motivate them to move in the direction which you believe to be the correct one.

When you are interviewing, you are listening to someone else's statements and, through face-to-face communication with him, asking questions which will help you determine whether you are satisfied with his statements. The word "interviewing" is used here in a broad sense to cover all those situations in face-to-face communications where the interviewer's job is to listen and obtain information which will help him decide how to act. Interviewing techniques are useful in such varied situations as the employment interview, the problem-solving discussion, the disciplinary interview, the sales call, and the staff meeting.

The distinction between reporting and interviewing is essentially a distinction between giving information and receiving and analyzing information. There are frequently times in face-to-face communications when you must be both a reporter and an interviewer, but it is useful in this book to look at these two processes separately.

This Step 8 has five guides:

- *Chart progress on Purpose Vector.* This guide offers a simple means of charting the progress of face-to-face communications, primarily for interviewing but also for reporting.
- *Use your spare listening time.* This guide emphasizes a key principle for effective listening.
- *Listen for poker chip structure.* This guide emphasizes a key technique for effective listening.
- *Watch for and use nonverbal signals.* This guide applies to both listening and speaking.
- *Plan and rehearse the formal talk.* This guide applies to the more formal one-way oral presentation.

The first guide in this step—Chart progress on Purpose Vector—offers a simple means of charting the progress of face-to-face communications.

The next two guides—Use your spare listening time, Listen for poker chip structure—apply to listening alone.

The fourth guide—Watch for and use nonverbal signals—applies to both listening and speaking.

The fifth guide—Plan and rehearse the formal talk—applies to the more formal one-way oral presentation.

CHART PROGRESS ON PURPOSE VECTOR

Introduction

Face-to-face communication is a fleeting thing; when the words are spoken, they are gone (unless someone is recording them). Later on, if you seek to analyze or review the meeting or the conversation to determine what went wrong or right, it is often difficult to do so because you have no way of charting the intangibles of oral communication and thus of identifying the process.

The Purpose Vector offers a simple means of charting the communications process in face-to-face communications. It

is so simple that with a little practice anyone, whether sender
or receiver, can use it mentally during face-to-face communication to help him see where the conversation is going and
thus help him decide what to do or say next. The Purpose
Vector looks like this:

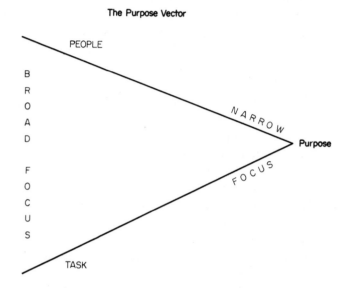

The Purpose Vector

In simplest terms, the communications process involves a
sender who transmits a message orally or in writing, and a
receiver who reacts to it and may transmit his reaction as
feedback:

In face-to-face communications, the sender usually transmits his overall message in a series of message units, to each
of which the receiver reacts with positive or negative feedback or no feedback. Each message unit may be as short as

one or two words or, sometimes, as long as the entire message. In the formal oral presentation or in the written message, a key distinction between face-to-face communications and oral presentations or written messages is in the timing and amount of feedback. In face-to-face communications, if the sender is listening and watching for feedback as he speaks, he will probably change later units of his overall message to reflect the feedback he received from earlier units.

It is this communications process that can be charted on the Purpose Vector. The best way to explain the Purpose Vector is to show how it is used.

Using The Purpose Vector   To use the Purpose Vector, start by answering the first People Question—What is your purpose? Enter your answer, as sender of the message, in abbreviated form under "Purpose" at the small end of the Vector. Your purpose may be a broad goal for an entire meeting or a much narrower goal of presenting a particular point of view at one moment in a conversation.

Next, using appropriate symbols, locate your first message unit within the Vector. To do this, decide whether it is broad or narrow focus in terms of achieving your stated purpose, whether it will probably have a low or high impact on the receiver, and whether it is people- or task-oriented.

Then, show on the Vector whether the receiver's feedback to your message is positive or negative, strong or weak, people- or task-oriented.

If you are using the Purpose Vector to chart the communications process in a group, also show if a particular message unit helps or hinders the group in completing its task, or helps or hinders the group in maintaining its group existence.

Finally, observe how the Purpose Vector will often demonstrate a new theory of leadership—namely, that leadership is shared, it is something that people do, and it shifts back and forth according to the subject matter under discussion and the willingness of members of the group to accept a change in leadership.

Three examples will illustrate the use of the Purpose Vector. The detailed process described here is neither necessary nor desirable in your day-to-day use of the Vector, but it is necessary to explain its use initially.

The Tardy Employee — I

Bill has noted that his subordinate, Sam, has been consistently arriving a half hour or more late to work in the morning. This pattern has persisted for several days, but Sam has said nothing to Bill. One morning, when Sam is again late, Bill realizes he must speak to him now, despite Sam's excellent record as a competent manager who handles customers well. Listed below are a series of opening statements or questions by Bill and a series of possible answers by Sam.

Opening Questions or Statements by Bill

1. "How's everything going, Sam?"
2. "Sam, you've been late recently. How's everything going?"
3. "Sam, why have you been late recently?"
4. "Sam, this is a warning. Stop being late."

Possible Answers by Sam

A. "Glad you asked. I've got a problem at home."
B. "Oh, pretty good."
C. "Fine, just fine."
D. "Isn't my work satisfactory?"
E. "Do I have to punch a time clock?"
F. "Yes sir."
G. "I quit."

Where do these questions, statements, and answers fit on

the Purpose Vector? To answer this, first determine Bill's purpose and enter it on the Vector, under "Purpose." Let's assume as the conversation starts, that Bill's purpose is simply to find out why Sam has been late. This is abbreviated "Why Sam late?"

In terms of this purpose, question 1 ("How's everything going, Sam?") is broad focus because it does not directly relate to Bill's purpose; it is people-oriented because Bill is asking about Sam as a person; it probably has a low impact because it does not appear to threaten or challenge Sam. Question 1 therefore belongs at the broad-focus left end of the Vector, near the top, or People, side, with a relatively short arrow pointing toward Purpose. The Vector now looks like this:

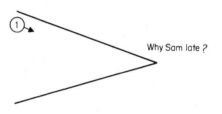

Next, look at several possible answers that could have been given by Sam. Answer A ("Glad you asked.") would mean that Sam has recognized Bill's purpose, has accepted his broad-focus, low-impact opening, and is prepared to explain the problem. In this case, the Vector shows this by a strong arrow aimed directly at Purpose:

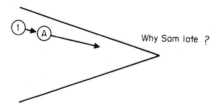

Answer B ("Oh, pretty good.") is much less satisfactory from Bill's viewpoint in achieving his purpose. Sam seems to be resisting here. If he understands why he is being asked the question, this answer does not show whether he is prepared to tell Bill his problem. Thus, answer B is shown with a thin zigzag line of resistance blocking the arrow:

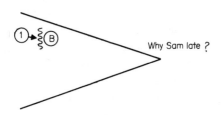

Answer C ("Fine, just fine.") would be a normal answer for a polite exchange between two people, but here it suggests definite resistance on Sam's part to discussing his problem with Bill. The resistance line here is heavier. There are no arrows attached to either B or C because Sam suggests no alternate in either case.

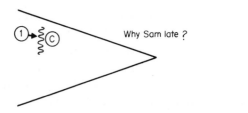

Answers D to G are less likely, in response to Bill's broad-focus, low-impact question 1.

Question 2 ("Sam, you've been late recently. How's everything going?") belongs in about the middle of the Vector. The focus is narrower. The impact on Sam will probably be stronger since an answer is expected. The possible range of answers to question 2 again include A, B, and C, but also now include D ("Isn't my work satisfactory?") and perhaps E ("Do I have to punch a time clock?"). D and E are shown on the Vector by stronger resistance lines.

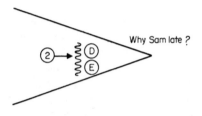

Question 3 ("Sam, why have you been late recently?") is clearly narrow-focus and high-impact. Answer A is still possible although B, C, D, or E seems more likely.

Statement 4 ("Sam, this is a warning. Stop being late.") — note that this is a statement and not a question — must be located next to the narrow right end of the vector. Bill is no longer asking for reasons; he is simply issuing an order. Sam's choice of possible answers is restricted. D and E are possibilities, as are F ("Yes sir.") and G ("I quit."):

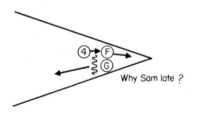

The Tardy Employee—II

In this example, the Sam and Bill exchange is carried further, starting with question 1 and answer B. Key exchanges in the conversation proceed as follows (Bill's questions or statements are numbered, Sam's are lettered—the numbers and letters do not correspond to those used in the first example).

1. Bill: How's everything going, Sam?
A. Sam: Oh, pretty good, I guess.
2. Bill: Just pretty good, you say. You did a fine job on the Wilson project, you know, but perhaps that put you behind on the other projects.
B. Sam: Thanks, Bill, but that's not the problem. I've caught up with the backlog. Everything is fine now, except for some technical difficulties on the Hillsdale project. I've been talking these over with Tom Jones. Perhaps you'd like to hear about it?
3. Bill: If you need my help, let me know.
But did you say you had another problem?
C. Sam: Well, Bill, I guess there is something else. It's a personal thing and I didn't want to bother you.
4. Bill: Go ahead, Sam.
D. Sam: Our son just dropped out of college, in midterm. He came home suddenly two weeks ago, and now he's just hanging around the house. He's upset everything. We've been having arguments far into the night.
5. Bill: I see. That certainly can be upsetting.
E. Sam: Yes, and that's why I've come in late. Overslept after arguing until 2 A.M. I guess you were wondering.
6. Bill: Yes, I was, Sam. It was beginning to be noticeable.
F. Sam: O.K., Bill, I get your message. You've given me an excuse for cutting out these endless arguments. I'll be on time again.

The above conversation is charted on the Vector as follows:

The Purpose Vector

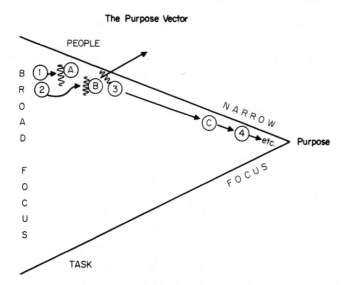

Question 1 is a broad-focus, people-oriented, apparently low-impact opening. Answer A shows mild resistance, which Bill goes around in statement 2 by repeating Sam's words without comment and then by praising him and suggesting a possible reason. In B, Sam shows willingness to continue the conversation, does not accept Bill's suggestion as to the reason, and then, in the last two sentences, attempts to aim the conversation toward his own different purpose (outside this Vector).

In 3, Bill doesn't buy that and brings the conversation back on track, aiming at his original purpose. This is now a narrower focus and a somewhat higher impact. In C, Sam accepts this. In 4, Bill encourages him, and then, in D and E, Sam tells his story, with an encouraging remark by Bill in 5 and then a somewhat firmer remark in 6.

Sam's final statement in F resolves the problem in a straightforward manner satisfactory to both parties. This happy resolution is convenient here in order to show how the

Purpose Vector can be used to record the key points in a complete conversation. The conversational exchanges recorded here are intended only to be those key statements or questions that represented a definite movement toward or away from the purpose of the conversation. (These key points could be called the blue chips in the conversation.)

Remember that face-to-face communications is conversation with a purpose. The Purpose Vector is therefore convenient in recording those key points in the conversation in which something is said that clearly moves the conversation toward or away from the purpose of one or more of the participants in the conversation.

The next example shows the use of the Purpose Vector in charting the course of face-to-face communications where more than two people are involved; following this example is a discussion of how the Purpose Vector can help you in everyday situations.

The Problem-solving Meeting

The added points in this example are the interaction between the various people and their questions or statements directed either at solving the problem (i.e., the task) or at maintaining the group as a group. The facts are as follows: John, the boss, has called a meeting of his three managers, Tom, Dick, and Harry. The time is Monday at 10 A.M. John has just learned that an important rush job promised for Friday afternoon will not be delivered until Tuesday morning.

1. John: I've called this meeting to find out what went wrong last week. Why didn't we get that job out? As you all know, it was a big one. I'm going to have to explain to the executive vice-president what went wrong. And you all know him; he wants results, not excuses.

2.   I'm turning this meeting over to you fellows

now; I'm going to sit and listen while you figure out what went wrong.

3. Tom: I don't see why we need a meeting. If Dick's people had finished the test results on schedule, the job would have gone out on time.

4. Dick: Cut it out, Tom. You're always trying to pass the blame on to someone else. Your people make mistakes, too.

5. Besides, we couldn't help it. The supplier didn't deliver the collars for the widgets until Thursday. There was no way we could've finished the job Friday.

6. If you ask me, John, you haven't got the right people in this room. Let's get some of those guys from Purchasing. They figured they could save the company a few bucks and make a big name for themselves with the comptroller by giving the order to that new supplier.

7. Harry: I think maybe Dick's right, John. How can we do our job if the supplier doesn't deliver on time?

8. John: Just a minute, fellows. Before you try to pass the buck to Purchasing, let's make sure our own house is clean. Tom, when did you first know we couldn't make the deadline?

9. Tom: Well, let's see. I guess I first sensed trouble on Thursday, not only because of the widget collar. We were having real trouble getting all the paper work straightened out.

10. Dick: I've got our work flow chart here, the one we use for every job. We saw problems as early as Thursday, but we couldn't do anything about it. Not in our area.

11. John: That chart looks like a good idea, Dick. Does this go with the job, or do you use it in your department only? Tom, Harry, do you use this chart?

12. Tom: No.
13. Harry: No.
14. John: It looks to me as if we have a communications problem right in our own area. Two of you saw the problem coming and kept the news to yourself. I want the three of you to get together and design a work flow chart that will give us advance warning of delays. Then maybe we can prevent problems like this from happening again.

In message unit 1, John summarizes his purpose as "What went wrong? You tell me," and then, in 2, states that he will listen while the others talk. He is thus setting a broad purpose for this problem-solving meeting.

Tom's answer, in message unit 3, shows resistance to the need for a meeting, while at the same time he suggests a task-oriented solution.

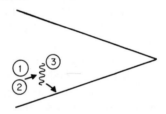

Tom's statement obviously has high impact on Dick, so Dick, in 4, reacts with strong resistance. In 5, he suggests a task-oriented solution and, in 6, attempts to pass the buck to Purchasing. The arrow here moves to the left and out of the Vector since Dick's solution would break up the meeting. In 7, Harry seconds Dick's suggestion.

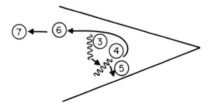

In 8, John now steps in, resists Dick and Harry's efforts to pass the buck, and in the last sentence brings the meeting back on the track.

The meeting now stays on track, as Tom and Dick move the meeting along toward its stated purpose, in 9 and 10.

Statement 11, however, is unexpected. John is now apparently changing the course of the meeting by reasserting his role as chairman and boss; in 14, he goes further by stating his belief as to the cause of the problem and the remedy. In doing this, John has discarded his original purpose, so that, starting at 11, the arrow goes outside to a new Purpose Vector.

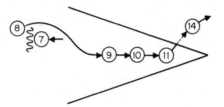

How the Purpose Vector Can Help You   The use of the Purpose Vector has been explained above in detail, taking each message unit in the three examples step by step and charting it on the Vector. You will find this process valuable and necessary in learning for the first time how to use the Vector.

Once learned, however, you would seldom need to chart in such detail. Thereafter, the advantage of the Vector is that it gives you, in any face-to-face communications situation, a quick means of visualizing (mentally or on paper) the progress of the conversation toward the sender's apparent purpose, and helps you decide what to say next. You can now answer the first People Question by saying to yourself—I want my statement or question to have a high impact or a low impact; to be people-oriented or task-oriented; I want to change my purpose; I want to get definite feedback, etc.

In using the Purpose Vector in discussion with others, precise agreement is not necessary as to the symbols to be used. Avoid becoming bogged down in detail. Consider the Purpose Vector rather as a useful tool in mentally charting progress of a conversation and, in particular, in noting a change in the course of the conversation or in deciding, if you are the sender, the type of remark you want to make next.

Several specific suggestions follow for day-to-day use of the Purpose Vector:

Selling — If you are a salesman or sales manager, use the Purpose Vector to chart a sales call. Record on the Vector those key moments when the prospect reacted favorably or unfavorably to a statement you made; record your opening in terms of focus and impact; show whether you used a closing that effectively zeroed in on your purpose. This process will often help you identify weaknesses and strengths in your presentation.

Proposing — If your superior has turned down a proposal you made to him, review the progress of your conversation on the Vector. Was your purpose clear? Would it have helped at any point if your focus had been broader or narrower, your impact higher or lower? Should your approach have been more people- or task-oriented? Note that a point-first opening will usually be narrow-focus, task-oriented.

Instructing — If your subordinate reacts poorly to your instructions, are you being too much of a Theory X manager, using a narrow-focus, task-oriented, high-impact approach? If so, back off the next time and start with a broad-focus opening. On the other hand, if your subordinate's work is not up to what you regard as proper standards, are you being too much of a Theory Y manager, using a broad-focus, people-oriented, low-impact approach? Should you close in and clearly set out for him the standards you require him to follow?

Problem Solving — If someone comes to you with a problem, he starts by reporting it to you, and therefore you become the interviewer. Do you have a tendency to jump in the middle, express your own opinions, and attempt to push your point of view?

Will you be more successful if you back off and use the broad-focus, low-impact questions that are typical for a nondirective approach? If you keep doing this until you know the problem, you then will be sure you know your own purpose. After that, you can start to move in toward the narrower end of the Purpose Vector, sharpening your questions and statements.

If you feel you are less effective in face-to-face communications than you would like to be, whether in interviewing or reporting, and if you feel it is important to improve your skill in this area, then consider enrolling in the kind of human relations workshop that offers role playing, problem solving with unstructured small groups, or even sensitivity training. These processes are used in unthreatening laboratory situations to help participants not only gain valuable insight into themselves, but also see which approaches are effective and which are not in face-to-face communications.

Charting Shifts of Leadership on the Purpose Vector   The traditional view of leadership has been that it is a constant, belonging to some people and not to others, and that somehow the traits or abilities that result in leadership can be collected in a list of absolutes, valid at all times and places.

The Purpose Vector helps demonstrate the validity of a newer theory of leadership, namely, that leadership is shared, it is something that people do, and it shifts back and forth according to the subject matter under discussion and the willingness of members of the group to accept a change in leadership.

For example, in The Tardy Employee—II, unit B, page 198, Sam asserts leadership by attempting to steer the conversation in another direction. In 3, Bill rejects this and retains leadership. In unit 2 of The Problem-solving Meeting, page 200, John deliberately turns the leadership over to the group. Dick asserts leadership in message unit 6 by attempting to pass the buck to Purchasing. In 7, Harry follows Dick's leadership, but John, in 8, refuses to accept this. Later, in 10, Dick tentatively asserts leadership by mentioning his flow chart. John accepts Dick's assertion of leadership here by picking up the flow chart idea, and then John resumes leadership by asking the others to adopt the flow chart.

The pure Theory X manager never relinquishes leadership and thus never really listens to his subordinates except as they report to him within his preset framework; to do so would constitute a challenge to his leadership and authority. In such case, leadership does not shift. This is equally true of any meeting where the chairman of the meeting is in firm charge and, for valid or invalid reasons, is not listening to questions or statements or accepting advice or challenges to his leadership. By contrast, the Theory Y manager consciously relinquishes leadership when he seeks advice or delegates authority. (This does not necessarily mean he weakens his ultimate authority as boss.)

Use the Purpose Vector concept, therefore, to help you identify assertions of leadership (your own or someone else's) whenever any group of two or more people are in face-to-face communication.

USE YOUR SPARE LISTENING TIME

Are you an effective listener? Test yourself on these ten questions,[18] answering them yes or no:

1. Does your mind wander off on mental excursions while you are listening?

[18] Based on similar questions suggested in Ralph G. Nichols, and Leonard A. Stevens, *Are You Listening?* New York: McGraw-Hill Book Company, 1957, p. 160; by permission.

2. Does something you hear turn you off, so that you stop listening?

3. Do you stop listening because you feel the speaker has nothing worthwhile to say?

4. Do you puzzle over the meaning of the speaker's words as you listen?

5. Do you concentrate on facts, rather than structure?

6. Do you stop listening if the speaker is difficult to understand?

7. Do you fake attention while your mind wanders?

8. Are you easily distracted by the speaker's appearance or actions?

9. Are you easily distracted by outside sights or sounds?

10. Are you an elaborate notetaker?

If you are a good listener, your answer to every one of these questions should have been no; but don't be unduly alarmed if you were honest enough to answer several of these questions yes, or to recognize that your answer could depend upon the person you are listening to and the surrounding circumstances.

These ten questions are a useful checklist of some common listening faults. Here is a brief summary of the problem or problems underlying each of these questions:

1. There are many reasons why your mind can wander off on mental excursions. Several of these are discussed in detail in this Step 8.

2. The effective listener, aware of his own prejudices, does not allow them to interfere with his listening.

3. Psychologists tell us that we are all prejudiced in favor of those who are most like us and against those who are most unlike us; an awareness of these prejudices helps us communicate more effectively.

4. If you puzzle over the meaning of the speaker's words, you will soon fall behind in your listening.

5. Listen for the poker chip structure rather than for those

facts or examples that illustrate the structure. This technique is discussed in the next guide.

6. If you stop listening because the speaker is difficult to understand, you are a lazy listener. You may have been spoiled by too much TV watching, which requires very little sustained listening effort. Commercials drive the message home in short, repetitive bursts; the content of many programs requires little intellectual effort.

7. If you fake attention while your mind wanders, you may well be hurting no one but yourself. A typical example of this is the college student who appears to be absorbed by the professor's remarks but allows his mind to wander far away. This bad listening habit is a specialized example of the mind wandering covered under point 1, but deserves separate mention because it is so common.

8 & 9. Effective listening is hard work. Listen for the poker chip structure and don't allow yourself to be easily distracted.

10. The problem here is similar to that in point 4. If you take elaborate notes, you will fall behind in your listening. Brief outline notes which record in a few key words the speaker's blue chips and red chips are generally all the notetaker has time for.

Since few of us have been trained in effective listening, it is no surprise that we are not good listeners. Only a few schools and colleges provide adequate listening training. Yet, of the four communication skills, writing, reading, speaking, and listening, most managers spend substantially more time listening than they do writing, reading, or speaking. Estimates of the average time a manager spends listening vary from 40 to 60 percent of the working day.

If you question this, keep track of how much time you actually spend in listening, speaking, reading, and writing during the next week. You may be surprised to find how much time you spend listening.

Can you learn to listen effectively by reading a book on listening or by reading the even briefer discussion in this and the next two guides? Probably not, but by reading about listening you can become aware of how poor most people are as listeners and of the need for listening training. This awareness in itself is a big step forward and will start you down the road to being a more effective listener.

The first of the ten questions above reveals the most important reason why many of us are not effective listeners. The question asks if your mind wanders off on mental excursions while you are listening. Most of us, if we answer honestly, would have to admit that frequently our minds do wander.

Why? It does little good to simply say that we are not paying attention or that we are not concentrating. That is obvious, but it does not solve the problem to be told to pay attention or to mentally berate ourselves for failure to do so. The answer is that (1) effective listening is hard work, and (2) we think much faster than we talk.

The computer in your brain can process words at a much faster rate than anyone is able to speak these words. Psychologists estimate that the brain can process words at from 600 to 1,200 words per minute; but most people speak at about 120 words a minute. So, you have spare listening time between the speaker's words to use your mind for thinking.

What do you do with this spare time? This is the key to effective listening. If you use your spare listening time to listen more effectively to what the speaker is saying instead of wandering off into excursions that are less work mentally than the process of effective listening, you have already taken the most important step toward better listening.

Why is effective listening hard work? To listen effectively requires careful, orderly, organized thinking about the speaker's message. For the same reasons that developing a good poker chip outline for a written or spoken message is hard work, it is hard work to concentrate on the speaker's message, to pay attention to what he is saying, and to organize his ideas in your mind along with your own reactions to his ideas. How much easier it is to turn off your mind and allow it to wander off into less-taxing excursions—plans for the weekend, that new mini-skirted secretary, the items on the desk or table in front of you, anything, in short, to avoid concentrating on the business at hand. Yet, the spare time is there. To listen effectively, learn to use this time effectively.

LISTEN FOR THE POKER CHIP STRUCTURE

How do you use your spare listening time effectively? The answer is surprisingly simple—listen for the poker chip structure of the speaker's ideas. What are his blue chips; subordinate to each blue chip, are there any red chips? Unless you are taking notes or unless you have a trained memory, you will not be able to remember more than perhaps two blue chips and one or two red chips under each blue chip; but if you can develop your listening ability even to this point, you will have made real strides toward effective listening. (A widely used three-hour effective listening program concentrates almost entirely on identifying the poker chip structure of the speaker's ideas. The program of course does not use the term "poker chips" but rather refers to the main ideas and supporting ideas, etc.)

To help yourself find the poker chip structure of a speaker's ideas, quickly review mentally the three People Questions as you start to listen:

- What is your purpose as listener? If you can answer this question as soon as you start to listen, your listening will be much easier because you will know what to listen for.
- Who is the speaker? What do you know about him? What is his environment? What is his relationship to you? Who else is listening? What do you know about them?
- What does the speaker want? What action or result does he seek from you or others?

Next, as you listen, watch for the motivators which the speaker may suggest to help persuade you to act his way.

With this information in mind, then watch for his blue chip and red chip ideas.

If the speaker has organized his message carefully and shown you a visible structure, you will have much less difficulty in listening effectively because his poker chip structure will be obvious.

To help yourself identify the poker chips, try to organize the speaker's message as he talks. Find the blue chips; remember them by a few key words. Distinguish between the facts or examples and the principles underlying these facts. Principles are blue chips; the facts or the examples are almost always red chips. The fact or example by itself may be interesting, but you are looking for the principles behind it. Remember the facts or examples only if they help you remember the principles. Listen selectively. If the speaker is telling a story to illustrate one of his blue chip points, you don't have to listen as carefully as you do when he states the principle itself.

Ignore distractions no matter how tempted you may be to divert your mind to the distraction. Effective listening is hard work.

If it is important to you to understand fully what the speaker said, take notes, but keep them simple. If your notes become at all elaborate, you will fall behind and lose the speaker's thought, so don't bother with Roman numerals and capital letters. You won't need them for this kind of an outline, and they are distracting. Instead, show subordination of ideas by indenting as you write on the page.

If the speaker angers, annoys, or bores you, beware of a natural tendency to stop listening and turn him off.

If you are preparing to answer or comment on something the speaker has said, beware of the tendency to stop listening as soon as you decide it is your turn to speak. You become so concerned with finding the right moment to say something that you stop listening and may miss an important thought.

WATCH FOR AND USE NONVERBAL SIGNALS

Listen with your eyes for nonverbal signals, whether you are speaker or listener. Use nonverbal signals, as speaker, to help get your message across.

We are all familiar with the more obvious nonverbal signals. If, while I am talking to you, you start to fidget with the papers on your desk, tap your feet on the floor, and look out the window, you are giving me a clear nonverbal signal of impatience. If I disregard your signal, I do so at my peril.

Every good salesman knows the more obvious nonverbal buying signals. If you are the salesman and I am the prospect, if during your sales presentation I have been sitting back in my chair with my legs crossed looking at you doubtfully, and if I suddenly uncross my legs and lean forward in the chair, then my change of position may well be a clear buying signal.

Suppose you are the listener watching me as the speaker. My message is orderly, appropriate, and seems to make sense to you, but all the time I am talking, I am drumming my fingers on the chair, shifting my feet back and forth, and avoiding eye contact with you. Clearly I am nervous. In addition, the lack of eye contact suggests I am afraid to look you in the face for one reason or another.

These examples are obvious; others are more subtle.

Physical appearance provides important nonverbal signals. What kind of shirt and tie is a man wearing? What kind of dress, skirt, or pants is a girl wearing (e.g.,—mousy brown dress, black satin hot pants, faded dungarees)? Are the colors bright or subdued? How about the shoes (or lack of them), the length of hair, the concern or lack of concern for an attractive appearance. If you see this person regularly, how does all this compare today with the physical appearance of the same person yesterday? What about the eyes and the mouth? Does the other person look tired? Are the lines drawn around the mouth?

Some people are more skillful in reading these signs than others. It is largely a matter of practice and of paying close attention to all possible signs that will tell you, if you are the sender, whether your message is getting across in the way you intended; or, if you are the receiver, whether the sender's true message is different from the message presented by his words alone.

When you are the speaker, you can also take certain steps to present your message more effectively. These are nonverbal signals because they relate to your method of presentation, rather than to the words themselves:

1. *Show enthusiasm.* A vigorous, enthusiastic speaker who obviously believes in his subject and makes this clear to his audience is always more convincing. If by nature you are somewhat quiet, so that enthusism doesn't come easily, consciously practice it. Express your words forcefully and with stronger emphasis.

2. *Smile.* A sincere smile relaxes you and your audience. Don't be afraid to smile; don't be afraid to be friendly. A sincere, friendly smile is the oil that helps keep the contact points of human relations moving easily.

3. *Act confidently.* Don't walk into a meeting like a dog with its tail between its legs and slip into an inconspicuous corner seat, head down, with a grim expression on your face. When you do that, you are telling everyone that you feel like an underdog, and therefore you can expect to be treated like an underdog. When you act confidently, it helps you to feel confident; and when you feel confident, you improve your chances of success.

4. *Look your audience squarely in their eyes.* Lack of eye contact is a strong nonverbal signal that tells your listener either that you have no confidence in yourself or else that

you do not dare look him in the eye because you are not telling the truth. Also, without eye contact, you handicap yourself because you have no way of judging whether you are getting your message across effectively. You need the feedback that eye contact provides you.

5. *Use your hands.* Use them naturally and freely to emphasize or explain your words. The speaker (whether in face-to-face communication or in a formal talk) who uses his hands effectively is more interesting, usually more forceful, and, through the use of his hands, can help convey his meaning more effectively to his audience.

6. *Check your physical appearance in the mirror before you start.* What will this appearance say about you? Is this the message you want to convey?

PLAN AND REHEARSE THE FORMAL TALK

To prepare a formal talk, follow the People and Structure steps exactly as if the talk were to be written. Answer the People Questions, decide the motivators you want to use, and then build a poker chip outline.

The best structure for most formal talks combines point first and point last and is summarized by the oft-quoted advice—Tell them what you're going to say; then say it; then tell them what you said.

Be sure your opening catches and holds attention; be sure your closing is strong. Plan the opening and closing carefully; if either is weak, you risk not achieving your purpose.

Don't write out your talk and then read it word for word. There is no better way to put your audience asleep. (The rare exception to this is where the speaker must use exactly the right words; in that case, practice in reading aloud is essential.)

If you are delivering a technical paper at a professional convention, don't read the entire paper. Instead, deliver an interesting fifteen-minute summary. Those who want full details can get a copy of the full paper later and, in any case, will have to get a copy if they want to use your work.

Deliver your talk from your poker chip outline. Rehearse the entire talk at least once. Include enough detail on your outline so that you won't lose your way, but don't include so much that you start to read it. Do include, however, opening phrases that will help you get started on each new idea as you move through your talk.

When you rehearse, time yourself carefully. Be prepared to prune ruthlessly if your talk is too long.

If you are preparing an oral presentation to a client, to a customer, or to a group within your own organization, anticipate interruptions after the first few minutes. Better still, ask for questions and objections. By doing this, you receive essential feedback that tells you if your ideas are getting across. Plan your outline so that in the first one or two minutes (no more) you will summarize the key facts and recommendations (and expected benefits); then, if the interruptions are frequent or people must leave the meeting, you will not leave listeners in doubt as to your key points.

The few suggestions in the above paragraphs obviously will not make you an accomplished speaker, but they do not stand by themselves. Rather, these suggestions build on the People and Structure steps and the BRISLEDITCH guides of Step 5.

If your job will involve you in the making of frequent formal talks—whether oral presentations in a business setting or after-dinner speeches—then by all means enroll in a program that will give you actual practice and coaching in effective public speaking—there is no substitute for such training. Such programs are particularly valuable if the video tape recorder is used (closed-circuit TV) so that, through instant replay, you can know how others see and hear you.

On the other hand, no amount of skillful delivery, poise, or confidence can make up for a failure to answer the People Questions correctly; a failure to use motivators intelligently; and above all a failure to develop a tight, clear, carefully organized poker chip outline for your talk. Particularly in the business presentation, your audience is listening for meaning and structure. They must decide if they are prepared to take the action you want them to take.

Visual Aids

A final word in this guide concerns the effective use of visual aids — movies, TV, slides, transparencies on an overhead projector, flip chart, chalkboard. When properly used, visual aids can be enormously helpful to you in making your presentation more effective. But know how to use these aids correctly. Too many speakers do not. These tips may help:

1. A visual aid is just that — an aid to you in making a better talk. Don't rely on it to give the talk for you; use it only as an aid.

2. Keep your visuals simple! This rule (and it is a firm rule) is widely ignored, always to the detriment of the speaker.

3. If your visual contains words, either read aloud every word of it to your audience before you comment on it or give each person a handout duplicating the visual.

- Nothing is more distracting to an audience than the speaker who shows a visual full of words or complex charts, and then starts to talk about it without reading it and explaining it first.

4. Be sure the people in the back row can read every word of every visual. If they can't, don't use the visual or else provide a handout.

5. A few carefully chosen, simple, well-organized visuals are far more effective than too many, poorly arranged, cluttered visuals. Don't use a visual simply for the sake of using a visual — be sure it fits smoothly into your presentation.

6. Rehearse your talk with your visuals. Be sure your cues for each visual are clear.

7. Know your room and seating arrangement. Be sure all your audience will be able to see every visual. Check out the lighting arrangements and the location of the screen. If you are using a projector, have a spare bulb handy.

8. If you are using a chalkboard or flip chart, do not talk while you are writing on the board or chart. Your back is facing to the audience and they probably won't understand you.

Reinforcing for Results

IMPROVING YOUR SKILLS

What can you do as a manager or professional to improve your own communications skills? How can you apply the Behind the Words system to help you reach this goal?

Before answering these questions, it will help to review the Morris Maxim and the six hard facts, presented in the introduction as a summary of the increasing problems of poor communications; the Behind the Words system is the means for your attack on this problem.

The Morris Maxim says:

Communications problems grow much faster in any organization than the organization itself grows.

The six hard facts that lie behind the Morris Maxim are these:
1. Managers and professionals do their jobs by communicating with people.
2. Our educators have not taught us how to communicate successfully.

3. The autocratic structure of an organization causes increasing communications problems as the organization grows.

4. Because of poor communications, senior managers of large organizations lose the power to change the mindless, relentless onward movement of their organizations.

5. These communications problems daily become more serious because our increasingly complex world demands increasingly large organizations to manage it.

6. Improving communications is everyone's job; managers and professionals at all levels must
   - recognize the full implications of poor communications
   - attack the problem repeatedly
   - anticipate stubborn resistance to change

If you are ready to attack the problem, this closing section shows you how you can apply the Behind the Words system to improve your own communications skills.

Your six-minute appraisal

Do you want to apply the Behind the Words system to your own day-to-day communications, so that you can improve your own communications skills? If this is your objective, then reading this book is the first step in a process of behavioral change that will not take place overnight.

To get the further results you seek, reread the preview of the Behind the Words system at the end of the introduction. As you do so, note the list on the inside front and back covers of this book. It shows the steps and guides in the Behind the Words system. Use this list as a reminder of the system and as a reminder to you to apply these principles.

One more simple but most important step is required—your six-minute daily appraisal.

Starting today, plan to spend six minutes every day appraising the communicating you have done during that day in terms of the Behind the Words system. Preferably do this with a pencil and paper at hand. List the two or three most important communications situations in which you were involved during the day. Remember your list can involve writing, reading, speaking, listening, or any combination of these —the situation could involve a meeting; a face-to-face discussion with a superior, subordinate, or associate; a sales call; the preparation of a lengthy written report; an important letter to a customer; or the reading of a difficult report or letter written by someone else.

For each situation, ask yourself honestly whether you handled it well. Whatever your purpose was in this particular situation, did you feel you had reasonably achieved this purpose? If your answer is yes, then use the Behind the Words system to help you identify what you did well; if your answer is no, then use the Behind the Words system to help you identify what went wrong.

Start with the People Questions. Was your purpose clear from the start? Did you consider carefully the other people involved in this communication? Did you know and consider what they wanted? Did you use motivators appropriately; or, if you were listening or reading, did you recognize the motivators that were offered to you?

If you were the sender of the message, did you build a sound poker chip outline that helped your audience understand your message; if you were the receiver, did you recognize the poker chip structure of the message?

Was the structure of your message visible? Did you avoid continuous narrative, show meanings through word order, follow the Clear River Test?

Did you follow the BRISLEDITCH guides? Did you follow the steps for writing effectively, reading effectively, listening effectively? Does the Purpose Vector help you identify any particular areas of strength or weakness in your handling of this communication situation?

The answers to these questions will obviously vary materially according to the communication. But, if you take as little as six minutes a day to jot down on a piece of paper the two or three communications situations most important to you in the previous twenty-four hours, if you look through the Behind the Words steps and guides on the inside cover as you do so, and if you critically ask yourself which guides you followed or did not follow, then you will help yourself analyze both your own strengths and weaknesses and the strengths and weaknesses of others.

Try this same process at home, too. If you had an argument at home, ask yourself what went wrong in terms of the Behind the Words system.

If you find it awkward or inconvenient to appraise yourself while at the office, then mentally review key communications situations in terms of the Behind the Words system as you head home at night. In the beginning, however, you'll find it easier to do this with a pencil and paper and the list in front of you. Your notes can be as brief and cryptic as you want them to be; they're only for yourself. But a few notes will materially help you, particularly when you start using the six-minute daily appraisal.

To improve your own communication skills, you should develop a consistent, daily self-appraisal process. The process suggested here is simple and short; anyone can afford six minutes a day for a purpose as important as this. Remember, if you do communicate more effectively, you will be more successful in achieving your purposes. The six-minute daily appraisal will work for you if you will honestly appraise yourself and be prepared to overcome your own resistance to change.

Index

Advanced Green When Flashing, Case 3, 37–38
Army, the, as organizational model, 6, 56, 57
Audience:
  know your, 14, 25–28, 32, 33, 35, 37
  captive, fallacy of assuming you have a, 43–44
  negative hidden, 26, 36, 48

Backlog in Customer Service, The, Case 4, 45–50
Behind the Words system, 4, 9, 11, 21, 83–84, 121, 145–146, 180, 218–221
Behind the Words triangle (People-Structure-Action), 11, 21, 59, 143, 145
Bellugi, Ursula, 104n.
Brevity, need for, 147–149
Brisleditch guides, 18, 145–167, 215, 220
  be brief, 147–149
  be clear, 159–161
  be direct, 154–158
  be human, 163–167

Brisleditch guides (*Cont.*):
  be simple, 149–154
  beware of unnecessary memos, 161–163
Bureaucracies:
  autocratic structure of, 56–57
  mindlessness of, 8

Captive audience fallacy, 43–44
Carroll, Lewis, 111
Case 1, The Friday Rush Job, 31–34
Case 2, No Job for Alice Green, 34–36
Case 3, Advanced Green When Flashing, 37–38
Case 4, The Backlog in Customer Service, 45–50
Case 5, The Leaky Plumbing Risers, 75–81
Case 6, The Repair Shop Requisition Form, 81–86
Case 7, Electric Power for Strong Manufacturing Company, 86–90
Case 8, The Poker Chip Outline of This Book, 90–91

BEHIND THE WORDS ®

a system for effective management communications

PEOPLE

1. *Ask the Three People Questions*

- What is your purpose?

- Who is involved?

- What do they want?

2. *Use Motivators*

- Catch and hold their attention.

- Show them the why.

STRUCTURE

3. *Build a Poker Chip Outline*

- Identify your poker chips.

- Arrange in appropriate sequence.

- Decide your opening and closing.

4. *Plan a Visible Structure*

- Avoid continuous narrative.

- Show meaning through word order.

- Follow the Clear River Test.